The Dinner Fix

Cooking for the Rushed

Sandi Richard

Scribner

New York London Toronto Sydney

SCRIBNER
1230 Avenue of the Americas
New York, NY 10020

First Scribner trade paperback edition 2007

SCRIBNER and design are trademarks of Macmillan Library Reference USA, Inc.
used under license by Simon & Schuster, the publisher of this work.

COOKING FOR THE RUSHED, THE DINNER FIX, THE HEALTHY FAMILY,
GETTING YA THROUGH THE SUMMER and LIFE'S ON FIRE
are trademarks of Cooking for the Rushed Inc.

Designed by Cooking for the Rushed Inc.
Manufactured in the United States of America

10 9 8 7 6 5 4 3 2

ISBN-13: 978-1-4165-4276-6
ISBN-10:   1-4165-4276-0

For information regarding special discounts for bulk purchases, please contact
Simon & Schuster Special Sales at 1-800-456-6798 or business@simonandschuster.com

Also by Sandi Richard
The Healthy Family
Life's on Fire
Getting Ya Through the Summer

To our reader and to our reader with diabetes
"Cooking for the Rushed - The Dinner Fix" is not a cookbook which claims to cater to the complex dietary needs of
a person with diabetes. The nature of this book is speed and nutrition. A large number of North Americans have some
form of diabetes; therefore we feel it is helpful to provide information, on food exchanges and food group values.

In view of the complex nature of health in relation to food and activity, this book is not intended to replace professional or
medical advice. The author and publisher expressly disclaim any responsibility for any liability, loss, or risk, personal or otherwise, which is incurred as a consequence, directly or indirectly, of the use and application of any of the contents of this book.

This book is dedicated to our friend.

Dave

(Ron's brother and my brother-in-law)

Dave would have been proud of this book.
He loved an eating experience almost as much as he loved being a firefighter. All the guys in
his platoon looked forward to the days he was cooking. Every time a new book came out, he
beamed with pride, cooked up a storm and literally hand sold more than many book stores!
We miss our friendship, our laughter and sharing our passion for great food. There's one thing
we're sure of, he's toasting us right now with a glass of fine port, held high,
with that huge grin and smiling eyes that say, "Way to go!"
We hear you buddy!

Table of Contents

          Green: Mexican Hamburgers
          Blue: Spinach & Cheese Ravioli in a Tomato Tapenade with Green Beans
          Red: Asparagus Stuffed Chicken with Hollandaise and Greek Salad
          Yellow: Red Snapper with Pineapple Salsa, Pecan Wild Rice and Asparagus
          Red Wings: Asian Meatball Soup, Baby Carrots and Dinner Rolls

          Red Wings: Japanese Grilled Chicken, Rice and Stir-Fry Veggies
          Blue: Creamy Noodle Bake with Spinach Salad
          Yellow: All Day Roast with Fries and Peas
          Green: Pizza and a Tossed Green Salad
          Yellow Wings: Salmon with Cranberry-Lime Sauce, Rice and Broccoli

          Red Wings: Soft or Hard Shell Tacos with Toppings
          Green: Tuna Tetrazzini with Corn and Peas
          Red: Dry Ribs with Couscous and Broccoli
          Yellow: Sweet Indian Chicken with Rice and Spinach Salad
          Blue: Chipotle Steak with Balsamic Reduction, Potatoes and Italian Veggies

Table of Contents

Table of Contents

Introduction

Who am I, Sandi Richard, to be an authority on meal planning? After all, I was the Chicken Finger Queen! Oh yes, I could justify anything I threw in the oven from a box. Only problem... I kept getting bigger, and my kids kept getting pickier.

One day 22 years ago, I was called home from work. Paige was sick and needed to go to the doctor. As I was driving to pick up both Dougie and Paige, I kept saying to myself, "Don't cry, don't cry, don't cry!" You see, I don't look that pretty when I cry. I get the red puffy nose which alerts the world in seconds that I'm a basket case! As usual though, I managed a strong, happy front for the kids. I arrived at the doctor's office, checked in and sat down. While my sick kids played in the germ infested toys, I picked up a magazine. A title jumped out like a beacon!

"Dinner time is the most stressful part of the day!"

I glanced down, hopeful that this was written by a woman, a kindred spirit who I could connect with, someone who would understand and relate to my hopelessness this very day! But, nope, it was written by a guy, a male psychologist! I couldn't believe the nerve, a guy would think dinner time is the most stressful part of my day! Hum, buddy, you just gotta follow me around for 24 hours, you'll see stress, hum!! My curiosity kept me reading. "North Americans treat dinner like everything else in their lives, just another chore." He continued to say, "If North Americans simply knew what they were eating for dinner ahead of time, it would remove much of the stress parents put on themselves AND it would take care of our eating problems in the meantime. OK, now he had my attention! He continued, "North Americans try to adopt all kinds of cultural eating habits and quick fixes. They want the magic pill, but they're forgetting something. Most other cultures see dinner as an intricate part of daily living. They look forward to dinner. As well, each culture has a certain lifestyle that goes along with the way they eat. People in many Asian and European countries walk and cycle almost everywhere! There in my seat, while the kids passed on their sickness to the other kids, God spoke to me...well you know what I mean!

I love hearing stories of how people came to be where they are. There is often some circumstance or some epiphany day. Well, this day was mine! My prayer is that one day this man will present himself and show me that article he wrote, because this was a day that changed my life!

So why did this affect me as it did? Remember I mentioned at the start that I was getting bigger? I wasn't huge by any stretch of the imagination, but I was going there! I was fat paranoid! I jumped on every diet revolution there was!

Introduction...(cont.)

In these last years when low carbs came back into style, I wanted to scream out to the world Noooo! That's right, came back into style! Do your homework. If you look at the history of low carb, low fat, food combining, GI, calorie counting, portion control, cabbage soup, grapefruit...shall I go on? You will discover that historically we just keep rotating diets. Oh they are more scientifically fancy, because now we can prove the diets work with fibre optics and C.A.D. technology. We can see how the human body reacts to certain foods. So why then are we the fattest people in the world? I believe, it's because "The Diet" never includes life!

The rose colored glasses came off that day. I realized I had bought into the ads, the beautiful skinny woman in magazines and on TV, the woman I desired to be. (...despite two snotty nosed children in tow!) I looked in the mirror and decided that very day, that I was who I was. That's what God gave me and it wasn't that bad, so I had better work with it!

I started to research some of the diets I had tried...because they really did work temporarily! I discovered something I had never noticed before. "For this diet to work effectively you will need to **drink water, decrease your alcohol consumption and exercise!**" Is that why I had so much energy once on a diet? Could it be? I had changed my food but I also adopted exercise, water and reduced my alcohol consumption. But when life got in the way and the crazy diet food had to go, everything else went with it! This began a fascination, which grew into a hobby, a hobby that would lead me to where I am today! **Eating forwards.**

I decided that if I knew what I was eating for dinner, it would be easier to balance my eating during the day. In order to do that, I would need to plan my meals. PROBLEM!

I realized my biggest weakness took place about two and a half weeks into a diet, so I needed a system where I would do the work once and never again, 'cause what I didn't have, was time to meal plan!

I needed food that tasted good. I needed stuff I could buy at the grocery store...and I needed to drink more water, include food my family would eat and move my butt!

This is my fourth book in the "Cooking for the Rushed" series and I've never looked back! OK, so I looked back! I would have never imagined that my life would take this kind of a twist, and it all started because Paige got sick and I almost lost it!

Book Beginnings

I Was In A Story and Didn't Know It!

So how do you go from an epiphany day to writing books 10 years later? I loved everything about meal planning. I could have had the worst day, yet if someone asked me about a recipe and meal planning it was like someone plugged me in to life.

One day, after having a good old sob about my job, my beautiful husband looked me in the eyes and said, "It's just money, honey!" He went on to say, "You light up like a light bulb any time someone needs help with meal planning, so just go for it!" What Ron meant by, "Go for it!" was my dream of writing a meal planning book, helping families to learn what I had learned so many years earlier. But how could I? I didn't have a clue where to begin. I was flat broke and knew that 90% of authors don't succeed making a living with their writing. So why me? What would set me apart? To make matters worse I wanted grocery lists in the book. I couldn't take the chance that someone would purchase groceries for the week and then find their family didn't like the food. That would spell instant disaster! The average family would have to like 85% of the recipes. But considering the average cookbook only has a few recipes that a person repeats (for their family), how could I find out if people liked 85% of my recipes? The world is full of fantastic cooks and chefs and there are already a million different kinds of cookbooks out there. What made me think I could develop enough recipes with that kind of success rate? Seven kids of my own with different likes and dislikes didn't hurt, but I needed much more than that. I needed to figure out a way to test the food with real families on-the-go.

Our First Big Blow

Ron and I love our morning routine of sitting in bed with a coffee. We pray, give thanks and plan our day. We solve the world's problems, sort out teen's moods, plan building projects but for some reason it took us forever to figure out how we could test the food. Then one day Ron and I had a brain wave. I would make up meal kits and deliver them to offices downtown. It would be an alternative to grocery shopping for families two days per week and they could rate the meals. I would cut the meat, make the sauce,

wash the lettuce or veggies, but they would need to cook the meal, because I needed to know how things turned out when they were in charge of the cooking. Surely, within a year, we would get the results we needed to create a book, like no other. We told everyone we knew we were writing a meal planning book (big mistake). We confidently went with our plan to the health board to have our kitchen approved and got our first big blow. The health board would not approve our kitchen; in fact it became obvious that the house we were living in would need far too many changes to ever be approved. Ron's solution, we needed a different house.

Selling the House

Our house was worth $98,000 (and that's after sinking $5000 of renovations into it to make it sell) so how were we ever going to afford a house that could accommodate a commercial kitchen? We would need a very specific house. It would have to have an undeveloped basement and it's own entrance. This was one of the health board's requirements. The only houses that had undeveloped basements were in the newer neighborhoods. They were way beyond anything we could afford, especially now that we only had Ron's teaching income to live on. One Saturday, Ron decided that we were going to check out a few open houses. We visited 4 homes and none met with the requirements we needed. It was 5:00 P.M. with one home left to view. We walked into a very plain raised bungalow. It was dated but clean and the price was right, only $20,000 more than the home we were living in. But, it was in a well established neighborhood, so the basement was likely developed. We asked the realtor, "Can you show us the basement? This question often came out of our mouths before even looking at the developed level. (I'm sure all the realtors thought we were setting up some sort of drug grow-op in their neighborhood.) We walked downstairs and it was completely open. An undeveloped basement with huge beautiful windows and a door from the outside leading right to one corner. Within one hour, we put an offer on the house.

After the deal was signed, we wondered what the heck we were thinking. This wasn't just a dream anymore; we have seven kids and we just bought a house with an undeveloped basement! Were we insane? To make a long story short, we moved in, cashed retirement savings plans and anything else that wasn't strapped down to the floor. We needed to support a family of 8 (10 at one point, but that's another story) and build a commercial kitchen.

We worked day and night developing the basement. After the kitchen was ready, we got our first couple to try a test kit. After three weeks we still had one couple! But thank the Lord, within a few weeks after that we had people calling from all over the city asking about our service. I would explain, "It's not a service; we are testing for a meal planning cookbook." "Yeah yeah," they would reply, "but can you bring kits to our office?" We tested up to 160 servings per week for over four years, but the results by the end of the first year were depressing. We were nowhere near getting a book out. We were completely shocked with what people wanted to eat in the work week. If it wasn't for the smug comments from parents at the kid's sports events asking, "Wheeeen's the book coming out.. teehee?" we may have considered dropping the whole idea. It got to the point where I could barely get the meals out on my own. There was no way I could keep up that pace. I was shopping, prepping and delivering meals and I was still a mother of seven children! Ron had an idea; he would apply to teach three quarter time instead of full time to continue with the testing. Now I knew we were crazy!

Ron Quits His Job

The fairy-tale continues when Ron decides to apply to teach half time. Doug, the eldest who had graduated from high school was fascinated with the food industry, and asked to join us for a year to see if it was something he could sink his teeth into as a career. (He eventually decided, NO!) We had heart, soul, love, gusto and determination. What we didn't have was money, a publishing deal or for that matter a book!

No one would give us money. We even tried to take out a mortgage on the house but the bank wouldn't do that because Ron wasn't making enough money. Everything went on the line. The house, the savings, you name it…we just believed in what we were doing that much. We were also blessed enough to have one of the test families invest in the publishing, and the Business Development Bank lent us $25,000. Our personal bank finally agreed to a $30,000 line of credit (only because Ron cornered poor Stan, our banker, every day asking him to try a couple of our meal planning weeks!) Stan finally decided to get Ron off his back by trying it out and his family were immediately hooked! Soooo, we had some money. Now we needed to prove that we could sell books. We self-published our first three books in the "Cooking for the Rushed" series. The first book "Life's on Fire" was a national best seller within weeks. (At which point Ron springs it on me that he now wants to apply for a full time leave from teaching.)

The second book "Getting Ya Through the Summer" was a best seller in it's first week and so was our third book "The Healthy Family." When touring for "The Healthy Family" three different television network executives encouraged me to have my own show. I really loved the people I knew at one of the networks so was leaning that way, but soon after, a production company heard about my show concept and within a few weeks, and a big thumbs up from Food Network, a show was born. The rest is history!

What Drove Me Crazy About
Week Day Cooking and How I Fixed It

Prep Code
I wanted a book that visually told me how long I had to prep and when my family would be eating dinner! That way I could get groceries for the week, but choose a meal for each evening that matched the chaos (or not) of my life! I didn't always want to quickly make dinner and eat as soon as I got home. Sometimes I wanted to play with the kids and then eat dinner. Sometimes I had to do laundry ('cause the pile was too high to ignore), yet I still wanted dinner off my back. Sometimes I didn't even have time to chop before I needed to get my butt out the door. I created a color coded system, my prep code! **See Prep Code on page 37.**

Equipment List
I knew that half my problem was committing to making dinner after work. If I took all the equipment out before I had time to change my mind, I wasn't going to put it all back. Having an equipment list also guided helpers to take stuff out when I wasn't around.

Left to Right Format
At the end of a long work day, I was too pooped to read recipe ingredients and then try and match it up with the corresponding instruction in a paragraph below. You gotta be kidding! I was mystified why recipe books weren't written left to right.
I wanted the full ingredient list, but why couldn't each instruction be beside the coinciding ingredient. Hence my trademark left to right format!

Real Photos
I love it when I look at a cookbook, see a beautiful photo, get excited about making the dish and then some meatloaf turns out like soup. I wanted real photos. But I have to admit, no photos at all was also a bummer! I decided that our books had to have photos, real photos with no photography tricks. No hair spray, lard or blow torches, no glycerine or dye. Just food, real food that all of us would eat after each shot was taken. If the dish is ugly, I think the reader needs to know that ahead of time! (It may taste great but ya wouldn't want to entertain with it!)

Grocery Lists
I wanted to make sure ther were grocery lists for each week and that the grocery lists weren't just available in our books, but on our website as well, so that you could print them out!
Go to www.cookingfortherushed.com

Nutritional Data
Now what good is nutritional data for a single dish of, let's say, meat. I'm not going to just have meat, I am going to serve it with a salad and rice…you get the idea. So nutritional data wasn't real. I had to calculate and count, ooor, forget about it. Our books had to have great data, for the entire meal!
But people weren't used to following a recipe that included all the components for a meal. The starch, the veg, the protein…so that's why the recipes have symbols on the left. It lets you know, as you are reading, what part of the meal you're working on, at a glance! This also helps a person replace components if they want. *i.e. You have left over rice so you skip the starch.*

● = protein component   ■ = starch component   ▲ = vegetable or fruit component

All The Stuff That Can Screw Up Dinner

Diets don't work long term, meal planning does!
page 14

Meal planning for the 21st century.
page 16

What's love got to do with it?
page 18

Picky eaters aren't born,
parents create them!
page 20

Monster drinks!
page 22

How much should I prep ahead?
page 24

Family dinners,
are they really that important?
page 23

Diets Don't Work Long Term, Meal Planning Does!

Sandi, how can you say diets don't work?
When I was on my diet, I lost 5 inches off my waist!

Ahhhh, do you see the first flaw with the above sentence? A statement that I hear over and over! "WHEN I was on that diet…" Key word WHEN. Sometimes people even get mad at me when I say, "If that diet is so amazing, why aren't you on it anymore?" I think the reason people get angry is because they are defensive. They think that I am shining a spotlight on the fact that they didn't have the self discipline to stay on the diet. It's quite the contrary. In fact, I assume that most people can't sustain a diet; it's been proven over the course of history. If you have children, staying on a diet may even be impossible. Here's why! Even if all the scientific data in the world points to every logical explanation for why a particular diet will work, unless that diet includes LIFE you're likely setting yourself up for failure!

The real common sense diet must include family, schedule and lifestyle.

If it doesn't, you will not be able to sustain it without adversely affecting those areas!

So lets say you've gotten into the cycle of unhealthy eating, then dieting when you get fed up of looking and feeling tired. So if I am saying that diets don't work, what is a person to do? The first thing you do is simple. Make yourself a sign that says,

"We Are A Fix It Today and Screw It Up Tomorrow Nation."

Post this on your mirror and read it every morning! In other words, focus on long term results, because that is sustainable. I think we always start with food, because food seems like the easiest solution, and gosh, we sure don't have time to get off our butts! So the night before or in the morning be sure you know what you will be eating for dinner. YUP, That's it!!! Now there is a great lifestyle change to begin your journey!

And by the way…if you are a parent DO NOT discuss dieting in front of your children. From toddlers to teens you are programming them to diet just like mom or dad, despite how healthy they may be. If you don't believe me you can go to the internet and find long term studies on the topic yourself.

Now, I want you to close your eyes and think of what you ate in the past few days. The cycle for most people goes like this. Wake up scrambling. Grab coffee. Run out the door. Get so hungry that you don't feel well. Grab what's convenient. Go out to lunch. Grab what's convenient. Get home starving. Grab what's convenient. Time passes by before heading out. Grab what's convenient.

If you read about home organization, the best authorities will tell you, "Put the key rack in a location you tend to throw your keys. Why? We are creatures of habit. What in the heck does that have to do with food or meal planning you ask? Very good question. If we are creatures of habit, and statistics tell us that most of us have no idea what we are having for dinner each night until we walk in the door, how **could** a diet work? A diet radically changes a habit. And unless the entire family buys into the lifestyle change you are making, there will be one dinner for the rest of the family and one for you. Yea right, that's going to last a long time!

So if convenient describes the way we live now and we are creatures of habit, we must work with that...like the keys. We may need to redefine convenient, but it must stay convenient none the less. Knowing that convenience is a strong factor affecting our decisions, what makes us go there? We are too busy!

Most often in a family one person is the "asker" of the meals. That means someone is saying…, "What would you like for dinner?" What is the answer? When I speak at conferences and ask that question it blows my mind when an entire group, hundreds of people, simultaneously say, in a whining voice, "I DON'T KNOW!" They all burst into hysterics. Then I ask, "What happens once you give up asking and you choose the dinner yourself?" They all start whining words and phrases like, "I don't like that!!" They all laugh again. Shortly after the laughter, some even cry. Why? Vindication! They realize, maybe for the first time, they are not alone! The asker of the meals has been set up to fail!

When I ask men or women what it is about dinner that seems so hard, they inevitably say,

"It's THINKING about what to have for dinner."

Isn't that interesting! People tell me that if they don't have to think about what to make for dinner their life is easier, in fact a little more convenient! Aha, that fits right into our habits.

What if you put a sheet up on a bulletin board and told your family that you would stop nagging...I, I mean feeing overwhelmed if they could just write down dinner ideas and suggestions. Give them a whole week to respond, reminding them daily that if they don't choose, they will have to eat what they get. The whole family must be included, even the "asker" of the meals. That way the entire family can read what people's dinner choices are and that leaves room for discussion. The reason I suggest an entire week for this is so that we don't fall into the "fix it today, screw it up tomorrow" way of thinking. If it took a long period of time to create this problem, why would we think it could be fixed overnight. By chilling out and giving yourself a little extra time to fix a problem that was created over time, you have won half the battle.

After following the meal planning steps on the next pages, armed with meal information your family has given you, how can this change your life, your body and your mind?

Meal Planning for the 21st Century

If you know you are having a cheesy lasagna for dinner, will you eat that same thing for lunch? Not likely. So instinctively you will choose something different, when something is different it starts to balance your diet naturally, it becomes habit! Now that's convenient!!!

Once your body starts to change, once you feel more energy, once the family is more at peace, that's when you make little changes in activity. I tell you, this is not only doable and sustainable; it's actually the miracle pill we are all looking for!

Diets, for the most part, seem to be sustainable for just a few weeks. Repeat the meal planning exercise for a few weeks and life actually gets easier not tougher because you now have three weeks of workable grocery lists to rotate. Now that's convenient!

Five Basic Steps to Change Dinner Time Forever

1. **Tack a page on a bulletin board or fridge for family members to write their meal suggestions on, meals they will actually eat**
   …now that's convenient!

2. **Choose five meals based on your family's suggestions.**
   …now that's convenient!

3. **Create your master shopping list and place it in a sheet protector.**
   …now that's convenient!

4. **Use your master list to check which groceries you will need to buy for those meals**
   …now that's convenient!

5. **Look at your week's recipes each night to decide which meal fits your schedule the following day**
   …now that's not only convenient, that's when everything changes!

1. Tack a page on a bulletin board or fridge
for family members to write down
their **meal suggestions**.
Meals they will actually eat
…now that's convenient!

Use the blank grocery sheet at
www.cookingfortherushed.com
to create your masters

2. Asker of the meals sits down with tea or favorite relaxing drink and pulls out recipe books or cards for the five suggestions he or she will use that week. Give yourself a time limit to get the job done. **Write down the meals and which recipe book they can be found in.**

3. In the appropriate categories **list every ingredient** you will need to make those five meals. **I mean everything, as if you had no groceries in the house at all.** That way you always have a **master list** for that particular week and you will never have to make that list again.

Put that master list in a plastic sheet protector.

Put that in a small binder close to your recipe books and show everyone where it is.

On the back of the plastic sheet, don't forget to mark down the extra things you will need like toilet paper, dish soap, stuff like that. Use a washable marker.

4. Now that the list is complete aaaanyone can **check** to see **which groceries need to be purchased** for the week.

Once you know exactly what you have to buy, go get your groceries.

When you get home wipe the plastic sheet protector clean, put it back in your meal planning binder and put it back in it's place.

5. Every night choose dinner for the following night!

Each week you follow these steps you will have a new meal plan to add to your book.
On the weeks you don't have time, no problem, use one that's already done.

What's Love Got To Do With It!

L. BENNETT

Chicken or Fish is a whole chapter in a book written by one of my favorite comedians, Paul Reiser…a whole chapter…now why do you think that is? My guess is because it's an issue, ya think? In fact many comedians poke fun at the issue of dinner. So what's love got to do with it?

A parent is driving home after work. They can't wait to see their beautiful teen. They begin to daydream about when their child was young and how much love they have for them. They walk in the door and that beautiful teen has dumped the kitchen upside down! There are dishes in the living room and they are watching a TV show. They look up and say, "Hi mom (or dad), I'm starving, what's for dinner?" The parent is discouraged because once again they are going to look like a big grump. All the feelings they had just a few moments earlier fade because they feel hurt, abandoned and alone. The teen feels misunderstood; after all, they had a stressful day too! You can just imagine where a conversation like that may lead!

OOOR... A spouse gets home late; they have been caught in a traffic jam. They arrive home and see that their other half is home. They are saying a prayer that dinner has gotten underway but they walk in the door and nothing has been started. Ya think that person is going to get a big wet one and a smile? Nnnno...I don't think so! Now if this happens over and over, why on earth would a person attempt to make it home first?…and the cycle begins! OVER DINNER! Yup, it's happening everyday in North America. Parents are feeling guilty that they are not feeding their family food that is as healthy as it could be, as well as not spending enough time with them. Yet, when push comes to shove, they decide to trade their health for more time. If I bring home take-out food I get more time with my family and possibly avoid an argument, but no one wants to admit they've fallen into this trap!

When I speak at a conference, especially a woman's conference, I love to ask the following question. "How many of you cook dinner?" The hands go up like a great wave. Then I say, "How many of you feel ripped off that you are the only person figuring dinner out?" The hands go up with conviction! I follow with, "How many of you make dinner from recipes that are in your head?" The hands go up, but quickly fall and then there is a buzz of conversation in the room along with laughter. I say, "You see, if you are the cook, the organizer and the shopper and expect help, then you had better supply information on paper before you condemn them for not helping. Sometimes dinner can put someone over the top when they don't know where to start."

This makes some people angry. "So Sandi, you are saying that on top of cooking, organizing and shopping you want me to organize the planning as well? I have to teach them how to get involved on top of everything else?" "YUP, that's what I'm saying!" You can send me hate mail for saying that and keep it the way it is, or you can follow my meal planning steps and turn the whole thing around. If you decide to take the first choice, stubbornness will likely keep you exactly where you are. Hope you're having a good time!

Let's admit, over the past 10 years as a meal planner I hear more "true" stories about what people eat for dinner than you do. I have heard it all and dealt with tons of it on my show as well. Here's the deal, **many times, loving, caring partners really don't know where to start and that's it**. Really!

Remember taking math in school and the teacher would begin to teach a new mathematical method. There were always the odd kids, who sat there with that dumb look on their face. (I personally understood everything.) That student would ask the teacher to explain again. The teacher would explain, but in the exact way they said it the first time. I would remain puzzled... I, I mean, that student would remain puzzled and ask again. By this time the teacher is looking at the student like they have dropped their brains off at the door. The teacher can't understand for the life of them why this student doesn't get it. Well let me tell you why, it's 'cause the teacher does get it. Now, let's relate that to dinner.

One adult in the family knows how to cook, they know certain recipes work, they get it! Their partner stands there with this look on their face and the one who gets it keeps saying the same things over and over again. The person who knows how to cook didn't make much sense to the non cook in the first place, but the cook goes on day after day wondering why the other person doesn't get it! So the non cook goes through life as a math drop out....I mean dinner drop out, because no one taught them a different way. A way that starts slowly and becomes more rewarding... in small doses.

I will never forget speaking at this conference for dieticians. One came up to me later and said, "Sandi, my husband hasn't cooked for 30 years; he ain't going to start now!" I asked her, "Have you tried these exact methods." "Well no," she said, "but he just isn't interested, he doesn't want to cook and is quite happy with that."
I said, "Really, so your husband likes depending on other people?" "Well no," she said, "he's very independent!" I explained, "But cooking is simply a form of independence, so maybe you should tell him that!" I challenged her to try the meal planning steps with a sincere effort.

One year later I was speaking at another conference and guess who came up to me, meal planning book and all. YUP, her husband was not only cooking, but in her words, "He's an animal in the kitchen, I can't get him out. He even asked me to relay to you the little twists he has added to your recipes. He asked me to suggest you consider them because he thinks they are better now." Just a guess, but I bet they're having more sex this past year!

We were all raised in different environments with different responsibilities. Not everyone learned how to cook. But today's couple needs to work together.

And folks, that's what love has to do with it!

Picky Eaters Aren't Born, Parents Create Them

I'll never forget the look on my director, Neil Grahn's face, when I wanted to say on my Food Network show *Fixing Dinner*, "Parents create picky eaters, they are not born!" Weeeellll, I thought he was going to do a back flip on my head. Neil has two toddlers of his own.

Neil said, "My wife and I are not picky eaters, but our kids can be." I said, "Neil, I didn't say that if a parent is picky then the kids are (which I do believe to be true). I said parents create picky eaters." He continued to give me the *you are out of your mind* look. So I asked, "What do you do when you are exhausted and one of your kids refuses to eat what's in front of them? Do you let them dictate whether they eat it or not?" He replied, "Well, it depends. If they are hungry later we will make them something nutritious to eat." I said, Will that be something they like so that you don't repeat the hassle?" The lights came on and his *you are out of your mind look* suddenly disappeared. Neil and his wife don't do a lot of take-out and their kids for the most part eat pretty good. But Neil realized that day that all parents are struggling with the same issues, it just depends what you want to do about it.

I know parents want to please their children and their good intentions come from love.

It's an unkind decision in the long run to let your children dictate the food they eat.

Do adults like everything, NO! Will kids like everything? NO! But, as adults our choices don't usually boil down to grilled cheese, chicken fingers, fruit snacks, granola bars and fries (oh, sorry! I did forget to mention the #1 veggie eaten in America, ketchup) and by the way, it's a fruit!

Now why is it that most adults eat a greater variety of foods? Well, most middle aged adults came from families that didn't cater to what the children wanted to eat, so we learned to love some things and hate others. For those of us who almost threw up on the table because our parents insisted we eat all the peas…we have made eating more democratic for our children. The result, children will choose what tastes best, which isn't always healthy, and so for the first time in history parents may outlive their children.

I want you to think about this. We take our beautiful newborn babies to the doctor and we are overjoyed when they are in all the correct or above average percentiles for weight, height, learning, etc... We brag when it's great and are frightened when it's not quite right. When they have a fever we rush them off for a prescription, we sleep beside them so we can hear them breathing and then what do we do? We reverse it all by letting them choose what they eat. In the meantime we also reward them for poor eating habits.

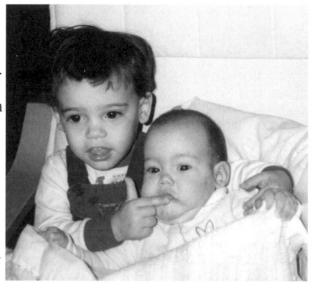

Yes, it's we. However unpopular that statement is, it's we! I know... I've been there! I remember when I decided to turn my eating life around. Dougie was two. I made home made chicken fingers. He turned blue, kicking and screaming, "I want the real ones!" referring to the deep-fried boxed variety he was accustomed to. Remember, I have seven children. When the kids were young some kids would eat anything. Two kids would have been perfectly content if they didn't eat any meat at all. One would have been thrilled not to see a veggie again in her life. Been there, done it, get it!!!

One Bite Rule

As the kids grew up, we enjoyed the results of the One Bite Rule. Everyone pretty much likes everything now with two exceptions; one child still gags at fish and one still doesn't care for onions. As you develop the One Bite Rule, it becomes apparent which dislikes are real and which are power struggles to get what they want.

Easy solution; make sure dinner includes a healthy component that you know everyone likes. The part they don't like, implement the One Bite Rule. Don't give in, because the most painful part will be the first little while...they'll get over it. If they don't eat the part they normally like, tell them that whether they eat it at dinner time or not, you still want to spend time

with them and hear about their day. If they say they have nothing to share tell them you want to share some of your day with them. Then wrap up what they didn't eat and pop it in the fridge (if there is any left after gabbing). When they are hungry later, warm up dinner. They begin to realize, the option is dinner...or dinner. Then you need to change your mind set, I am doing what is healthy for the child I love. "I'm not an ogre!"

Monster Drinks

Picky eaters aren't the only thing we should be worrying about with our youth. Have you seen the size of the drinks lately? And what's it all about when your favorite family restaurant keeps filling up the kid's glass of soda. We perceive this as value! Sure, that's what restaurants are in business for; to do you a favor and give you value…NO!!! They want to make money, so they provide a carrot, so that you will patronize their restaurant, because you perceive this as value! (I actually wouldn't mind so much if they really gave us a carrot.)

We have been trained, the bigger the meal the bigger the value! The bigger the drink the bigger the value. Well what if I told you that this thing we see as value is creating a situation where our children are showing early signs of heart disease. Diabetes has never been higher and we are seeing for the first time early signs of osteoporosis IN CHILDREN!

Is it OK for the kids to drink soda pop? Of course it is, in moderation, like everything else! As a matter of fact we finally told the kids that we really didn't want to spend the extra money on soda pop when taking them out for dinner as a treat! We asked them if they would mind ordering water and then we would buy them a large bottle to share after dinner at home. The kids thought we were big cheapos, and that was just fine by us! If they drank the soda from the restaurant, they easily could have each had the equivalent of 1 cup of sugar. But, because we chose to have them drink water at the restaurant, instead they might have as much as 32 oz of good old H2O. Then they would share a 32 oz jug (1 litre) of soda when we got home, in contrast 1 tsp of sugar each.

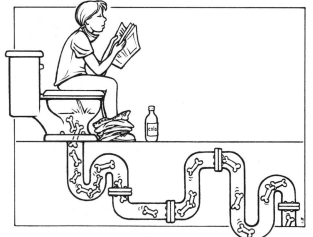

The phosphates in soda are like a magnet to calcium. If that's what kids are mostly drinking it's like they are peeing out their bones. If children or adults are drinking soda pop they better have a diet that is extremely rich in calcium. If you're not worrying about their bones, heart or diabetes, then consider this... They could consume a whopping 774 calories and that doesn't include what they're eating! That's just dinner! What are they drinking the rest of the day!

Parents, we gotta be in charge of this. They have a limited amount of time to build their bones. When they get jobs in high school and University, they will likely get enough soda to sink a ship, so for goodness sakes help them to limit what they are doing at home! Kids often eventually bounce back to what they are used to!

Family Dinners
Are They Really That Important?

When they were little, it was where they formed their eating habits. They learned good manners (at other people's homes). When they were in grade school, they proudly wrote of their family's tradition of eating together each night. When they were teens they always had something better to do than sit, eat and talk with mom and dad, but we forced them to anyways. It wasn't always pleasant, but is usually was. Sometimes we laughed, sometimes we fought, we shared, they tattled and it was completely intriguing listening to the varied reasons why they should get off dish duty each night! I did it so we would be healthy and I wouldn't get fat, but at the end of the day I got far more than I bargained for. I'm not a perfect mom and I have learned not to be the best housekeeper. I may have climbed over mountains of laundry, but we almost always ate dinner together as a family! We literally live meal planning.

Whether it's the Minnesota Institute for Public Health, Harvard University, or Columbia University, the findings are the same. Take a look at some of the studies on the topic and

then decide if you think it's important enough to try the meal planning steps to get dinner on track.

Teens that eat dinner regularly with their family are less likely to get involved in substance abuse and less likely to smoke cigarettes.

They are less likely to have weight issues. They are more likely to have higher grades. They are more likely to

feel their parents are proud of them. They are more likely to confide in their parents when it comes to serious issues Up to 40% of families do not eat dinner together 5-7 nights per week, yet 87% of families say that family dinners together are vital! That's a whole lot of parents feeling guilty!

The cartoon on the right appeared in our first book "Life's on Fire." My readers couldn't believe that I was insane enough to start the spaghetti fight! (Obviously they aren't my closest friends!) Well, the above picture is proof that it happened at least. It was our first and last food fight. (Who do you think was picking up the spaghetti noodles from every nook and cranny for a week?) As my eldest son, Dougie, would say, "Mom, you're not always the sharpest pencil in the box!"

How Much Should I Prep Ahead?

A question I am frequently asked is, "Should I make all my weekday meals ahead on the week-end?" Oh brother, why would you do that? We are already trading our health for time with our family. The reason we are in this predicament in the first place is because we don't have a lot of time. So you are asking me if I think you should take the little bit of time you have with your family to cook for hours? No! Look, if it's a social thing, if it gives you pleasure, if it fills your soul because you love to cook, by all means, go for it! But honestly, if you are cooking for hours on the week-end and see it as a chore, reevaluate what you are giving up, as that's the last thing a busy family needs these days!

I do believe in doing little things ahead, while you are already doing something else. Double things like spaghetti sauce, meatloaf, soups, stew, meatballs, lasagne or casseroles. Anything that freezes well and can be used as a back up meal!

 I am a big believer in a little preparation the night before. No more than ten minutes. This could be getting something ready for a crock pot meal. It could be cutting veggies for a meal that a preteen can assemble the next day, or it might be something as simple as browning hamburger or boiling potatoes. Most of these things can be done during the commercials of your favorite show.

If a recipe calls for half an onion, for goodness sake, chop the whole thing and freeze the other half. Finely chopped onions freeze beautifully. In fact just about anything can be frozen if done right. There is nothing like preparing dinner and realizing there is chopped onion in the freezer.

Other things you can do to make your life easier are to purchase larger quantities of steak, chicken or fish. Place them in a large freezer bag and separate the pieces so that each piece doesn't touch. Seal the bag and lay it flat to freeze. When you need to make a dish, it's very convenient to take out just what you need.

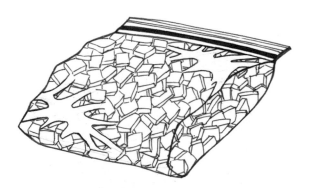

If a recipe asks you to thinly slice beef for a stir fry, slice double, lay a freezer bag flat, spread the meat out thin, seal it up and it defrosts it minutes when you need it. If you are cutting up bite size pieces of chicken for a stir fry or pasta sauce, do the same.

Always remember to lay the bag flat and spread the ingredients out thin before sealing. That way when it's fully frozen, it can either defrost quickly or you can separate all the ingredients by squeezing the bag from the outside. This makes it easy to pull out exactly what you need.

Making Dinner Easier

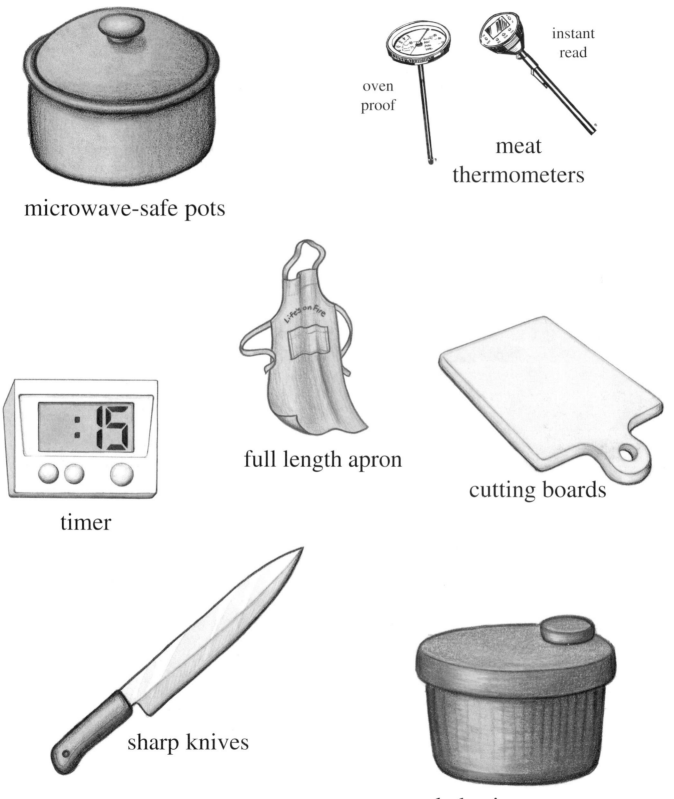

microwave-safe pots

oven
proof

instant
read

meat
thermometers

timer

full length apron

cutting boards

sharp knives

salad spinner

Making Sense of Instructions

Working with families is truly humbling. Not only do I remember the chaos I had to sort through, with getting kids to activities and working, but I also remember feeling dumb that I was far too pooped to read a recipe at the end of a long day at work. (whether that happened to be work in the home or out)

We recently did a show where the dad didn't like to cook because he found recipes intimidating. He didn't understand what things meant in a recipe. To make matters worse he was Spanish and therefore had a tough time working through some of the North American slang. Now this guy was no dummy. He is a university math professor. When I said to him, "Follow the recipe step by step,"…he was fine until he got to *toss in the mushrooms*. He asked, "What does that mean?" It hit me, some books say *toss in*, some say *throw in* and others explain it differently. I decided from that day on that I would look through a million cookbooks (very slight exaggeration) and try and explain some of these terms that we cooks now take for granted.

Cooking Lingo

Methods of How to Cut
Cut - Finely Cut - Chop - Dice - Julienne - Slice - Sliver

Cut	- often gives you an instruction afterwards to explain how to cut
Finely Cut	- to cut the ingredient into tiny little pieces
Chop	- to cut; it's just another way of saying it
Dice	- to cut something into cubes; the instruction will often tell you how big or small those cubes are to be. *This one can be confusing as the term sometimes replaces finely chop or finely cut. You'll need to use some common sense on that one, but it will often say finely dice.*
Julienne	- to cut very tiny lengthwise pieces
Sliver	- to slice thinly
Slice	- to cut; often you will be told how thick or thin to slice
Arrange	- to place an ingredient in or on something, often using your hands
Beat Egg or Beat Mixture	- to mix together fast using an electric mixer or whisk, recipe will often instruct you how long to beat, or what the texture should be like
Blanch	- to immerse veggies or fruit into boiling water and then, depending on how long you are to do that for, transfer them quickly to ice water or very cold water to retain their color and stop the cooking process
Blend In or Stir In	- anything with **IN** means add that ingredient to what you are making - to add and then stir it into the existing mixture

Combine — The sentence may say to combine the following ingredients. That will likely mean that it doesn't really matter what order you put things in. *After they are all added you want to stir until you are confident everything is well mixed.*

Drizzle — to pour an amount of liquid, ever so lightly, over something

Marinate — to soak something (could be meat, tofu, veggies etc…) in a particular liquid *This can be to flavor or tenderize depending what the ingredients are.*

Parboil — to boil something but not all the way *A recipe is requesting that you don't boil the ingredient all the way because the recipe needs that item only partially cooked to make the recipe work.*

Pat Dry — to take some of the moisture off with a dish towel or a paper towel

Preheat — to bring an oven or appliance to a certain temperature before cooking

Puree — to blend into a smooth mixture (no lumps) *Usually needs a blender or food processor or a very strong speedy arm that can move at the speed of light!*

Rinse — to put something under water and rinse it off, usually to take the dust off, i.e. dried beans, rice, fruits or vegetables *I like to rinse frozen veggies to rinse off any freezer crystals that may have collected. I also like to rinse my washed lettuce from a bag or veggies from a bag. (Call me crazy, but I don't know who touched them!)*

Seed(ed) — to take the seeds out or the seeds are gone

Soak — to bring moisture back into something that is dry or has been dried i.e. noodles, beans or dried mushrooms

Spread — to evenly distribute something either onto the surface of a pan or maybe over another ingredients

Toss — to stir this mixture like…an electric clothes dryer. *Make sure the ingredients from the bottom of the bowl are brought up to the top and continue until every thing is combined.*

Toss In, Throw In — anything with **IN** means add that ingredient to what you are making

Whisk — to use a fork or whisk to stir an ingredient or ingredients quickly. The tongs help to break up the ingredient(s)

Conversion Charts

All measures are not the same
These are a great guide, variances are minimal

Liquid Measure

1 oz	30 ml
2 oz	60 ml
3 oz	100 ml
4 oz	125 ml
5 oz	150 ml
6 oz	190 ml
8 oz	250 ml
10 oz (1/2 pint)	300 ml
16 oz (1/2 litre)	500 ml
20 oz (1 pint)	600 ml
1 3/4 pints (1 litre)	1000 ml

Dry Measure

	stand	exact
1 oz	30 g	(28.3)
4 oz (1/4 lb)	125 g	(113.4)
8 oz (1/2 lb)	250 g	(226.8)
12 oz (3/4 lb)	375 g	
16 oz (1 lb)	500 g	
32 oz (2 lbs)	1 kg	

Can and Jar Comparison

4.5 oz	127 ml
8 oz	227 ml
10 oz	284 ml
12 oz	341 ml
14 oz	398 ml
19 oz	540 ml
24.5 oz	700 ml

Oven Temperatures

	F	C	F	C	
	175 -	80	350 -	175	
	200 -	95	375 -	190	
	225 -	110	400 -	205	mod hot
very slow	250 -	120	425 -	220	
	275 -	140	450 -	230	hot
slow	300 -	150	475 -	240	
mod slow	325 -	160	500 -	260	very hot

Buying Meat or Produce

1/2 lb	225 g
1 lb	450 g
1 1/2 lbs	675 g
2 lbs	900 g
2 1/2 lbs	1125 g
3 lbs	1350 g

Measuring

	stand	exact
1/4 tsp	1.2 ml	
1/2 tsp	2.4 ml	
1 tsp	5 ml	(4.7)
1 Tbsp (3 tsp)	15 ml	(14.2)
1/4 cup (4 Tbsp)	55 ml	(56.8)
1/3 cup	75 ml	(75.6)
1/2 cup	125 ml	(113.7)
2/3 cup	150 ml	(151.2)
3/4 cup	175 ml	(170)
1 cup	250 ml	(227.3)
4 1/2 cups	1 litre	(1022.9)

Monitoring Your Fat (for the day)

Percent	If You Eat... Intake Should Be	Your Daily Fat
30%	1500 calories	50 grams
	2000 calories	67 grams
	2500 calories	83 grams
	3000 calories	100 grams
25%	1500 calories	42 grams
	2000 calories	56 grams
	2500 calories	69 grams
	3000 calories	83 grams
20%	1500 calories	33 grams
	2000 calories	44 grams
	2500 calories	56 grams
	3000 calories	67 grams

Adjusting Nutritional Data
To Your Specific Needs

- Most of the recipes in **The Dinner Fix** provide 4-6 servings.
- Our test families varied in size. Some families said there was too much food for 4 people, and others thought it was just right.
- If you have 4 adults in your home with very healthy appetites the meal will probably serve 4 (when we write *Serves 4-6*). Sometimes someone gets a left-over lunch the next day!
- If you have younger children the recipe will probably serve 6 (when we write *Serves 4-6*).
- When a range is given for the number of servings a meal makes, the higher number is used. i.e. When a meal says 4-6 servings the nutritional data assumes you are dividing every component of the entire meal into 6 portions. The nutritional data is for one portion of each component. This also applies to the food exchange and food group data.
  Use the formula below to adjust the nutritional data when we write Serves 4-6 and for your family it serves 4.

Adjusting Data when a Meal Serves 4 instead of 6

# of g fat x 1.5 = # of g fat
i.e. 12 g fat x 1.5 = 18 g fat
(12 g fat per serving for 6 servings) = (18 g fat per serving for 4 servings)

This formula works for all our nutritional data..

Weights and Measures

- Imperial and Metric conversions are approximate only.
- Occasionally we do not provide exact conversions so readers can identify with the can, jar and package sizes produced in their country.
- When weights or measures are provided in both Imperial and Metric, nutritional data is calculated using the Imperial measure.
- When a range is given for a measure, the first given is used to calculate nutritional data.
- When a choice of two ingredients are listed (i.e. chicken or pork), the first ingredient is used for nutritional data.
- Ingredients listed as optional are not included in nutritional data.
- Fresh garlic (from a jar) is packed in citric acid.
- Vegetables and fruits are medium size unless otherwise specified.
- Buns are 2 1/2 oz or 70 g and dinner rolls are 1 1/2 oz or 42 g

Diabetic Food Exchanges and Food Choices

A very large number of people have some form of diabetes, so we feel it is important to include this information as well as the detailed nutritional analysis. Our recipes have very high standards for taste, speed and nutrition. It seems only fair to allow a person with diabetes the luxury of being able to use a regular cookbook with great tasting meals. They can simply adjust components according to their specific dietary requirements. There is another very important reason for having food exchanges or choices. Some people use food exchanges or choices as a tool to monitor their eating habits for maintaining a healthy weight.

The **Canadian Diabetes Association** made changes to their meal planning system in 2004 and also Health Canada has regulated the Nutrient Value labels found on most food products. Together with changes to medications & methods of managing diabetes, the association has developed the **Beyond the Basics** resource for meal planning.

The goal of Beyond the Basics is to assist people to include a variety of foods, based on **"Canada's Food Guide to Healthy Eating"** and promote optimal diabetes management.

With information about carbohydrates people can keep their intake of carbohydrates consistent. A carbohydrate choice contains 15 grams of available carbohydrate (fiber is subtracted from total carbohydrate). Fruit, milk and starches are included in the carbohydrate choices. Vegetables are considered to be free when consumed in 1/2 cup (125 mL) portions.

The **American Diabetes Association's Exchange Lists** have also been revised recently. They have also developed the **Diabetes Food Pyramid** grouping foods based on their carbohydrate & protein content in order to keep carbohydrate content consistent. This new list helps one get more variety through a flexible eating plan.

Equipment List:

BBQ or broiler pan
BBQ tongs
Large stove-top pot
Small stove-top pot
Cutting board
Colander
Medium serving bowl
Sharp veggie knife
2 mixing spoons
Fork
Measuring cups and spoons
Aluminum foil

Per serving:

Calories	328
Fat	7.8 g
Protein	26.5 g
Carbohydrate	39.0 g
Fiber	4.9 g
Sodium	94 mg

U.S. Food Exchanges:		Cdn. Food Choices:	
2	Starch	2 1/2	Carb
3	Meat-lean	3	Meat/Alt
1	Vegetable		

Nutritional data, including food choices and exchanges are calculated for the entire meal (per serving).

Sodium content is included for the benefit of those monitoring salt intake.

Canada's Choices and America's Exchanges are included for each meal in our book.

GHEG - Beyond The Basics - Diabetes Food Pyramid
Comparison of The Estimated Nutrient Values

Food Groups	GHEG***	Beyond The Basics**	Diabetes Food Pyramid*
Carbohydrates		15 g carb	
Grains & Starches	15 g carb 2 g protein 0 g fat	15 g carb 3 g protein 0g fat	15 g carb 3 g protein 0g fat
Fruits	10 g carb 1 g protein	15 g carb 1 g protein	15 g carb 0 g protein
Milk & Alternatives	6 g carb 4 g protein 0-4 g fat	15 g carb 8 g protein variable fat	12 g carb 8 g protein 0-8 g fat
Other Choices	10 g carb	15 g carb variable fat & protein	other carbohydrates 15 g carb variable fat & protein
Vegetables	10 g carb 1 g protein 0 g fat	<5 g carb 2 g protein 0 g fat	5 g carb 2 g protein
Meat & Alternatives	0 g carb 7 g protein 3 g fat	0 g carb 7 g protein 3-5 g fat	0 g carb 7 g protein 0-8 g fat
Fats	0 g carb 0 g protein 5 g fat	0 g carb 0 g protein 5 g fat	0 g carb 0 g protein 5 g fat

***GHEG - the Good Health Eating Guide (& it's symbols) was used by the Canadian Diabetes Association until 2004
**Adapted from Beyond The Basics:Meal Planning, Healthy Eating & Diabetes Prevention & Management, ver 2, 2005/12/20
*Adapted from Exchange Lists for Meal Planning, American Diabetes Association, 2003

Equipment and More

When we say, **"Don't change yet! Take out equipment."** on the recipe, we're referring to don't change your work clothes. It's amazing how following this advice will reduce your stress.

The **Prep Code** to the right of the equipment list lets you know the "hands on" time required to prep the meal before dinner (pg 37), after taking out the equipment and ingredients.

A **Slow Cooker** under the clock is a reminder you must prep the night before or the morning of your meal, using...a slow cooker.

A **BBQ** under the clock lets you know at least one portion of the meal is grilled.

A **Crescent Moon** above the recipe alerts you to a 5 or 10 minute prep the night before. Most of these can be started the same day, in the morning, if your schedule allows.

Our **Celery Hugger** on the "About the Recipes" pages lets you know the meal is vegetarian or has suggestions on how the meal can be adjusted for vegetarians.

Tell me about Spices

Spices can be confusing, so here's the basic scoop.

Unless a recipe calls for a fresh spice or herb, they mean dried.

Dry Spices or Herbs
If the recipe says **leaves,** but it doesn't say fresh, it means dried, but not ground. Leaves usually have irregular shapes, like snow flakes, but reeealy tiny! If it says ground, the spice or herb has been ground into a powder. In some cases you can get dried leaves that are not crumbled or ground. This is simply to confuse us all. But have no fear; the most common are kaffir lime leaves or bay leaves.

What's the Difference Between Using Fresh Herbs or Dried?
Fresh are often, but not always, added at the end of a recipe or they can lose their flavor. Dry spices (if they still smell wonderful when you open the container) can really boost the flavor of dishes and they are stored easily which makes them super convenient.
Flakes usually mean dehydrated and these are most often onion, garlic and ginger.

The Confusion of Cilantro
Fresh Coriander is also known as cilantro or Chinese parsley.
Dried coriander can be found as whole seeds, whole leaves, flaked leaves or ground, so it's important to note what the recipe is asking for. Why? To drive us crazy!

Common Combinations
Chinese Five Spice Powder is a combination of Szechwan pepper, cassia, cloves, fennel seeds and star anise. So many people ask me if MSG is one of the five spices, it isn't.

Curry Powder (curry leaf is a herb and different)
Curry powder is not a spice. It's a combination of spices and perfect for most North Americans, authentic, but not really! You can usually purchase curry powder in mild, medium or hot. The difference is often in the amount of cayenne pepper. A standard curry powder may include some of the following ingredients: dried chillies (or cayenne), black mustard seeds, coriander seeds, black peppercorns, cumin seeds, ground turmeric, fenugreek seeds and ground ginger.

Garam Masala is a blend of roasted ground spices which include coriander seeds, black peppercorns, cumin seeds, bay leaves, green cardamoms, ground mace, cloves and cinnamon. You can leave out the bay leaves and coriander, but I like them in. The components in Garam Masala are often easier to find than it is at times. If your grocer has an ethnic section which includes foods from India or Africa you can often find it there. If you can't find it, use a pinch of each of the spices in it. It will be close enough. I do suggest that you try to find some, because you often don't need much and it really makes a difference.

Mexican Chilli Powder; 2 tbsp mild, medium or hot chilli powder, 2 tsp cumin powder, 2 tsp sweet paprika, 1/2 tsp salt.

Poultry Seasoning; 3/4 tsp ground thyme, 1/2 tsp ground sage, 1/2 tsp marjoram 1/8 tsp white pepper, 1/8 tsp ground nutmeg

Pumpkin Pie Spice; 1 tsp cinnamon 1/2 tsp ginger, 1/4 tsp nutmeg, 1/4 tsp ground cloves

Common Spice Blends

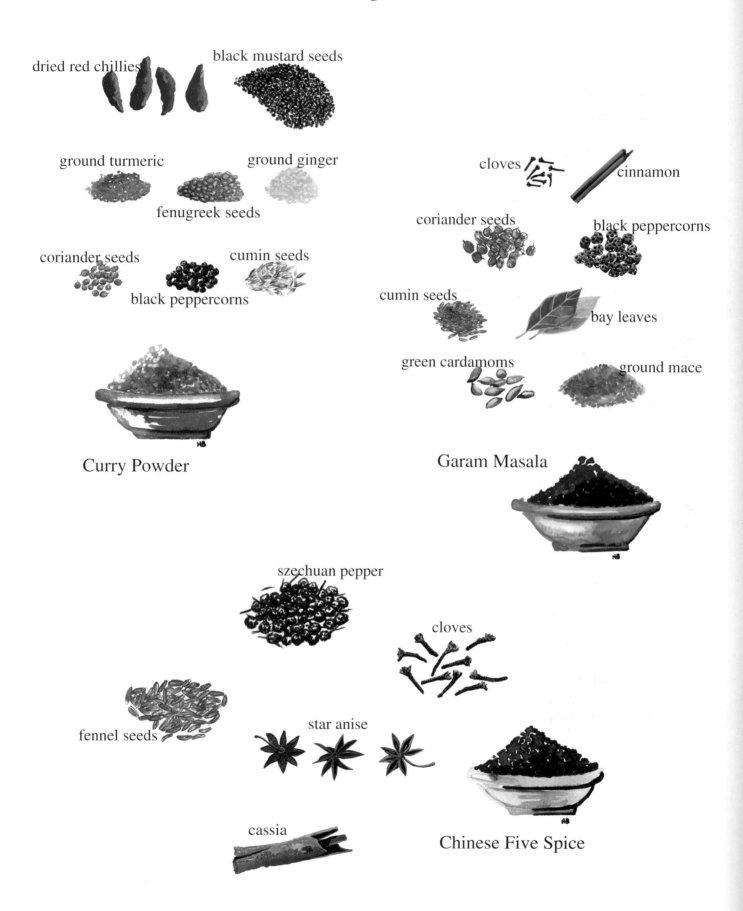

dried red chillies

black mustard seeds

ground turmeric

ground ginger

fenugreek seeds

coriander seeds

cumin seeds

black peppercorns

Curry Powder

cloves

cinnamon

coriander seeds

black peppercorns

cumin seeds

bay leaves

green cardamoms

ground mace

Garam Masala

szechuan pepper

cloves

fennel seeds

star anise

cassia

Chinese Five Spice

Cutting for Speed

How to cut an onion

trim one end:

cut in half:

peel:

follow the grain to sliver:

cut again to dice:

How to prepare asparagus

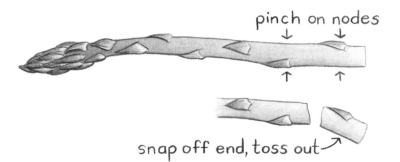

pinch on nodes

snap off end, toss out →

Chicken breasts are sold in two different ways

two breasts

one breast

How to cut green onion

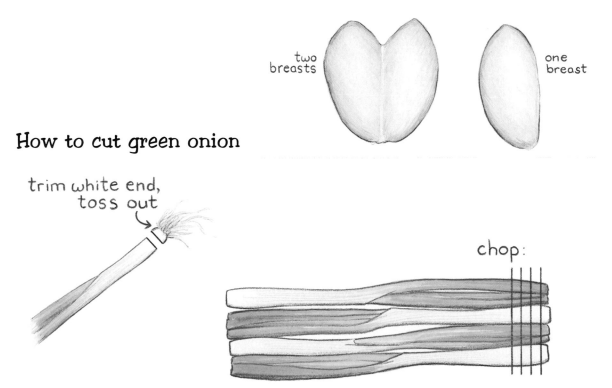

trim white end, toss out

chop:

Cutting for Speed

How to prepare lemongrass

peel back rough outside husk:

discard ends:

smash to release oils:

use only what you can finely chop:

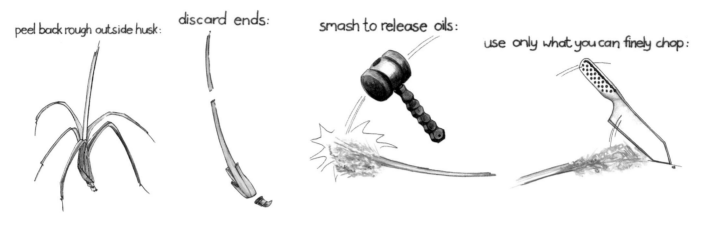

How to cut a mushroom

trim end, toss out

cut:

lie on flat side:

How to cut peppers

cut in this order:

1

2

toss out top and seeds

rough side up:

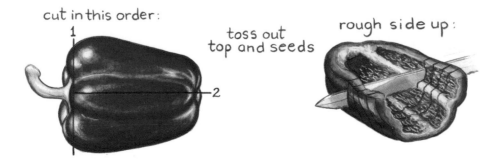

Food Guide Pyramid
A Guide to Daily Food Choices

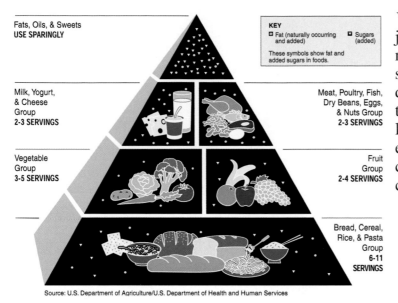

Fats, Oils, & Sweets
USE SPARINGLY

KEY
☐ Fat (naturally occurring and added)   ☐ Sugars (added)

These symbols show fat and added sugars in foods.

Milk, Yogurt, & Cheese Group
2-3 SERVINGS

Meat, Poultry, Fish, Dry Beans, Eggs, & Nuts Group
2-3 SERVINGS

Vegetable Group
3-5 SERVINGS

Fruit Group
2-4 SERVINGS

Bread, Cereal, Rice, & Pasta Group
6-11 SERVINGS

Source: U.S. Department of Agriculture/U.S. Department of Health and Human Services

The Food Guides... Out of Date?

You rarely hear a celebrity say, just follow the food guides! That's not cool! Celebrities have a responsibility to share only what is doable for the majority, or keep their opinions to themselves. Kids look up to them. If they say, for example, milk is bad, a young child who admires them may choose soda pop instead of milk.

The Food Guide Pyramid and Canada's Food Guide are just that... GUIDES!

The guides don't know how much exercise you get or how much money you have. They don't know anything about you, so they give everyone a simple guide to follow. Guides that are visual, clearly laid out and for the most part make sense. My eating habits tend to flip the veggie-fruit sections with the grains. If you cut our plates into three parts, half would be veggies. The other half of the plate would be split between protein and grains. That's how the guide works for me. Why? Because I only manage to exercise three times a week, and the rest of the time I am standing at a kitchen counter or working at a computer. My daughter Paige, on the other hand, played college basketball and now coaches high school basketball while she's finishing her teacher's degree, so she needs a few more grains than I do because she is far more active. You see, it's a guide!

We also have to look at the guide from a financial standpoint. When the kids were little I purchased far more things like pasta and bread because it was inexpensive and I had to make my dollar stretch. I was running from morning 'til night and as a sanity break had a brisk walk every morning, so I was able to burn off what I ate.

If we have common sense the guides work. You can't go heavy on bread and sweets if you're sitting at a computer all day, come home, then sit on the couch. You'll get fat! And if you have a really high metabolism, you may be skinny on the outside, but you're fat on the inside!

Health Canada   Santé Canada

CANADA'S
Food Guide
TO HEALTHY EATING

Enjoy a variety of foods from each group every day.

Choose lower-fat foods more often.

Grain Products
Choose whole grain and enriched products more often

Vegetables & Fruit
Choose dark green and orange vegetables and orange fruit more often.

Milk Products
Choose lower-fat milk products more often

Meat & Alternatives
Choose leaner meats, poultry and fish, as well as dried peas, beans and lentils more often

Canada

The Prep Code

RED and **YELLOW**

Less Cutting and Chopping

More Cutting and Chopping

It's time to eat in **30 minutes**
... when you need to get your butt out of the house fast.

**If either Red or Yellow have Wings,
it's time to eat in 25 minutes**

GREEN and **BLUE**

Less Cutting and Chopping

More Cutting and Chopping

It's time to eat in **60 minutes** or less
...when you have a small window of opportunity to prep,
but need to rush off somewhere while dinner is cooking,
or you want to relax before you eat.

MEAL PLANS

About the Recipes

Green

To make this recipe vegetarian combine all the spices in a small bowl, add Worcestershire sauce and 1 tsp of olive oil. Lightly brush on slices of zucchini, peppers, and large mushrooms, such as crimini. Once grilled add a little cheese for protein. Add all your favorite toppings, just like a regular burger. Yummy!!

Red Wings

This meal is easy and delicious! Our test families pointed out two things. The first is to make all the sauce. The proportion of sauce to pasta is great. The other thing is that you really need to wait until you're ready to eat before folding the sauce into the pasta, so it doesn't dry out.

Blue

I am not vegetarian so I looooove this meal with chicken. It's not only easy to make it's scrumptious and has an amazing presentation. If you are vegetarian, set your oven at 375° F. Butter slices of whole wheat bread and sprinkle with garlic powder. Spread mushroom soup on the unbuttered side and wrap the asparagus in the bread, butter side out and secure with toothpicks. Bake for 20 minutes or until golden. Serve with sauce and salad.

Yellow

This meal is something you would expect from a high end restaurant, yet it;s so simple to make. The presentation is out of this world. If you are vegetarian and eat fish, make this just the way it is or replace the fish completely by dunking a slice of firm tofu in flour, then water, then flour, then crushed pecans. Heat some peanut oil in a fry pan and saute until crusted on both sides.

Red

Yum! Yum! Yum! And sooo easy!! I love that I can make this in my crock pot and come home to a perfect meal full of protein, veggies included. Pair it up with a multigrain bun and it's like a good hug! Load this soup with one can of mixed beans (garbanzo, black and kidney) and veggies and it's the perfect vegetarian meal. It's absolutely delicious either way.

Week 1

Green: Mexican Hamburgers

> Our family rating: 9.5
> Your family rating: _____

Red Wings: Spinach & Cheese Ravioli
                     in a Tomato Tapenade with Green Beans

> Our family rating: 9
> Your family rating: _____

Blue: Asparagus Stuffed Chicken with Hollandaise
                     and Greek Salad

> Our family rating: 10
> Your family rating: _____

Yellow: Red Snapper with Pineapple Salsa,
                     Pecan Wild Rice and Asparagus

> Our family rating: 9.5
> Your family rating: _____

Red: Asian Meatball Soup,
                     Baby Carrots and Dinner Rolls

> Our family rating: 9
> Your family rating: _____

Mexican Hamburgers

Instructions:

Don't change yet! Take out equipment.

1. **Preheat BBQ** to med (approx 350° F) by starting both burners on a med-low setting.

2. Mix together beef, ketchup, Worcestershire sauce and spice in a large bowl
Form the mixture into 8 large patties, each 3/4 inch thick.

   These can be formed and frozen on the weekend to save time. Make sure you put parchment between the burgers, just in case you forget to take them out early to defrost.

   Place patties on **BBQ**. Close lid.
   Don't overflip, that's how the hamburgers break.
   Cook each side 5-10 minutes or until center is well cooked *Meat thermometer should read 170° F.*
   Rotate the burger once to create those beautiful grill marks. For cheeseburgers, place a slice of cheese on top of each hamburger for the last 3 minutes of cooking.

3. For the last 2-3 minutes of cooking toast the buns, cut side down, on the **grill**.

4. Slice tomatoes and onion and rinse lettuce leaves.

   Serve hamburgers on the buns with your choice of fixings.

   Mash one ripe avocado in a small bowl using a fork. Stir in 1/4 cup salsa.

Ingredients:

Take out ingredients.

2 lbs or 900 g ground beef (90% lean)
1/2 cup ketchup
1 Tbsp Worcestershire sauce
1 tsp freshly ground pepper
1 tsp chili powder
1 tsp cumin powder
1 tsp chipotle seasoning, salt free

8 slices light cheddar or Swiss cheese
  (optional)

8 multigrain hamburger buns

2 tomatoes
1/2 red onion
1/3 head leaf lettuce

ketchup, mayonnaise, salsa or
  guacamole (optional)

Quick Guacamole
1 ripe avocado
1/4 cup salsa (mild, med or hot)

Serves 6-8

35 Ready, Let's Eat

Equipment List:

BBQ (or electric grill)
Large bowl
Small bowl
Cutting board
Sharp veggie knife
Bread knife
Hamburger flipper
Stirring spoon
Fork
Measuring cups and spoons
Parchment paper

Per serving:

Calories	397
Fat	14.2 g
Protein	29.3 g
Carbohydrate	39.3 g
Fiber	3.8 g
Sodium	576 mg

U.S. Food Exchanges:		Cdn. Food Choices:	
2	Starch	2 1/2	Carb
3	Meat-lean	3	Meat/Alt
1	Vegetable	1	Fat
1	Fat		

Prep Time

Spinach & Cheese Ravioli
in a Tomato Tapenade with Green Beans

Instructions:

Don't change yet! Take out equipment.
1. Fill a large **stove-top** pot with water.
   Cover and bring to a boil.

   Combine salsa, pesto and maple syrup together
   in a small mixing bowl. Set aside.

   Add ravioli to boiling water and **reduce heat**
   to a medium boil. Set timer according to
   package directions. (approx 11 minutes)

   ...meanwhile...
2. Melt butter in a large nonstick **fry pan** at med-
   high.
   Add beans, lemon pepper and soy sauce.
   Toss to coat, then **reduce heat** to med-low.
   Stir often, until beans are hot, glazed and
   crunchy but tender.

   ...when timer rings for ravioli...
3. Drain ravioli in a colander.
   Heat tapenade mixture in the unclean pasta pot
   at med heat until hot.
   Return ravioli to pot and fold gently until all
   the ravioli is evenly coated.

   We love Parmesan on top.

   *Your kids will never know you are stuffing
   spinach into them. Yuuummmy!!!!*

Ingredients:

Take out ingredients.
water

Tomato Tapenade
1/3 cup salsa
2 Tbsp basil pesto (from a jar)
1 Tbsp maple syrup

3/4 lb or 350 g spinach and cheese ravioli
  (found in most deli or dairy sections of your
  grocery store)

Chef Style Green Beans
1 tsp butter

5 cups green or yellow frozen whole beans
  I like to blend both together.
1/2 tsp lemon pepper
1 tsp soy sauce, reduced-sodium

Parmesan cheese, grated (optional)

Serves 4

25 Ready, Let's Eat

Equipment List:

Large nonstick fry pan
Large stove-top pot with lid
Small mixing bowl
Colander
Stirring spoon
Large stirring spoon
Measuring cups and spoons

Per serving:

Calories	372
Fat	11.3 g
Protein	16.0 g
Carbohydrate	54.1 g
Fiber	5.3 g
Sodium	566 mg

U.S. Food Exchanges:		Cdn. Food Choices:	
2 1/2	Starch	3	Carb
2	Meat-lean	2	Meat/Alt
1	Vegetable	1 1/2	Fat
1	Fat		

15

Prep Time

Asparagus Stuffed Chicken with Hollandaise and Greek Salad

Instructions:

Don't change yet! Take out equipment.

1. Smear garlic on rough side of each chicken breast. Lay asparagus on top. Roll the breast around the asparagus. Secure with a toothpick.

   Heat oil in a large nonstick **fry pan** at med-high heat. Brown rolled chicken on all sides then add wine and chicken broth to pan. Simmer at med-high heat, uncovered, turning once, until liquid has almost evaporated. Cover and **remove from heat**. *Instant read thermometer should read 180° F.*

   ...while chicken is cooking...

2. Cut tomatoes and cucumbers into chunks. Place in a large serving bowl. Sliver onion and crumble feta, add to bowl. Add olives if you wish.

   Sprinkle spices all over, then drizzle with olive oil, lemon juice and red wine vinegar. Toss and let stand in **fridge**. Rinse lettuce in basket of salad spinner. Spin dry.

3. Beat egg yolks with a whisk in a small **stove-top** pot (no heat yet). Add lemon juice, dry mustard and Tabasco to yolks. Whisk together to combine. Melt butter, in a measuring cup, in **microwave** about 10 seconds. Very slowly drizzle the butter into egg yolks while whisking. then place on med-low heat. Slowly whisk in milk until smooth. Heat through while whisking. **Remove from heat.** *If you like your sauce a little runnier, add a little more milk.*

4. Serve this with multigrain dinner rolls *We don't, but you might like to.*

Ingredients:

Take out ingredients.
4-6 chicken breasts (1 1/2 lbs or 675 g)
1 tsp prepared garlic per breast (from a jar)
2-3 asparagus spears, per chicken breast
  (8-12 asparagus spears in all)
toothpicks

1 tsp olive oil (or cooking spray)
1/2 cup dry white wine (can be nonalcoholic)
1 can chicken broth, low-sodium
  (10 oz or 284 mL)

Greek Salad
3 Roma tomatoes
1/2 English cucumber
1/4 red sweet onion
3/4 cup feta cheese, crumbled
1/2 cup black olives (optional)
1/2 tsp lemon pepper
1 tsp oregano
1/2 tsp thyme leaves
1 clove garlic, minced (or fresh from a jar)
2 Tbsp olive oil
2 Tbsp lemon juice
1 tsp red wine vinegar
1 head red leaf lettuce

Healthier Hollandaise
3 egg yolks
2 tsp lemon juice
1/2 tsp dry mustard
1 tsp Tabasco sauce (optional)
1/2 cup melted butter
1/2 cup 1% milk

6 grainy dinner rolls
Serve the Greek veggies on top of the lettuce. Place a chicken breast beside the salad and drizzle with Hollandaise. YUM!!!

<u>Serves 4-6</u>

45 Ready, Let's Eat

Equipment List:

Large nonstick fry pan
Small stove-top pot
Salad bowl
Cutting board
Salad spinner
Sharp veggie knife
2 large stirring spoons
Whisk
Can opener
Corkscrew for wine
Measuring cups and spoons
Toothpicks
Instant read thermometer

Per serving:

Calories	531
Fat	29.9 g
Protein	37.3 g
Carbohydrate	31.2 g
Fiber	5.6 g
Sodium	566 mg

U.S. Food Exchanges:		Cdn. Food Choices:	
2	Starch	2	Carb
4	Meat-lean	4	Meat/Alt
3	Fat	3	Fat

20

WEEK 1

Prep Time

Red Snapper with Pineapple Salsa, Pecan Wild Rice and Asparagus

Instructions:

Don't change yet! Take out equipment.

1. Drain all the juice and 1/2 the pineapple into a small **stove-top** pot.
   Finely chop the whole onion, but only put half of what you chop into the pot.
   Add curry paste and stir.
   Heat on med-low until reduced to thick salsa.
   Remove from heat. Slice green onion adding to pot with balance of red onion.
   Stir and set aside.

2. Steam asparagus with water in a **microwave-**safe pot, with lid, at high 4 minutes. Let stand.

3. Combine rice and water in a large microwave safe pot with lid. Add chopped pecans and spice. Stir.
   ...when timer rings for asparagus take it out and put rice in...
   Cover rice and **microwave** at high 10 minutes, then medium 10 minutes. *Check package directions as cooking instructions vary.*

4. Heat oil in a nonstick **fry pan at med-high.**
   Drizzle fish with lime juice.

   Sprinkle fish with spices and flour on all sides.
   Saute each side of fish for 1-2 minutes or until slightly brown.

   Add wine and **reduce heat to medium.**
   Cover for 2-6 minutes, or until fish flakes through thickest piece with a fork. *If fish is thick it will take a little longer to cook that's why I give a range.*

5. Reheat asparagus in **microwave** for 1 additional minute before serving.

Ingredients:

Take out ingredients.

Pineapple Salsa
1 can unsweetened pineapple tidbits (14 oz or 398 mL)
1/2 of the whole red onion

1 Tbsp hot curry paste

1 green onion, sliced
other 1/2 of the red onion

20 asparagus spears (1 lb or 450 g)
1 Tbsp water

1 1/2 cups mixed rice (white and wild)
  I like Canoe brand
3 cups water
2 Tbsp chopped pecans
pinch (1/8 tsp) ground cinnamon
pinch (1/8 tsp) ground cloves
1/2 tsp Mrs. Dash Original seasoning

2 Tbsp canola oil
1 1/2 lbs or 675 g red snapper fillets
2 Tbsp lime juice

1/2 tsp basil
1/2 tsp thyme leaves
1/2 tsp salt
1/2 tsp pepper
1 1/2 Tbsp flour

3 Tbsp dry white wine (can be nonalcoholic)

30 Ready, Let's Eat

<u>Serves 4-6</u>

Equipment List:

Large nonstick fry pan
Small stove-top pot
1 lge microwave safe pot w/lid
1 med microwave safe pot w/lid
Cutting board
Sharp veggie knife
Stirring spoon
Fish flipper
Fork
Can opener
Corkscrew for wine
Measuring cups and spoons

Per serving:

Calories	414
Fat	8.9 g
Protein	29.7 g
Carbohydrate	53.9 g
Fiber	3.9 g
Sodium	385

U.S. Food Exchanges:		Cdn. Food Choices:	
3	Starch	3 1/2	Carb
3	Meat-lean	3	Meat/Alt
1/2	Fruit		

20

Prep Time

Asian Meatball Soup, Baby Carrots and Dinner Rolls

Instructions:

...the night before...
Take out equipment.

1. Fill a large **stove-top** pot with water and bring to a boil. Form ground beef into 1" tight balls placing into fully boiled water as you form. Set timer for 7 minutes after the last meatball goes into the water.

   When timer rings for meatballs, drain off the water and place the meatballs in the inner crock of the **slow cooker**.
   Add garlic, onion, ginger, pepper, soy sauce, chicken stock, and hot chili sauce. Stir, cover and store in **fridge** overnight.

   ...in the morning...
2. Return inner crock with cover to **slow cooker** and set on **low heat**.

   ...when you get home...
3. Fill a stove top pot with water. Cover and bring to a boil for noodles.

4. Slice green onions and add to **slow cooker**.
   Add snow peas.

5. Prepare noodles in a **stove-top** pot according to package instructions. Drain and rinse in a colander under hot water and set aside.

6. Wash baby carrots and set out on a serving plate.
   Combine mayonnaise, sour cream and spice in a small bowl.

7. Serve with dinner rolls.

   I like to place noodles in the bottom of serving bowls then ladle the soup over top. That way the noodles never get soggy!

Ingredients:

Take out ingredients.
water
1 1/2 lb or 675 g extra lean ground beef

2 tsp fresh garlic (from a jar)
1/2 onion, sliced
1 tsp fresh ginger (from a jar)
1 tsp ground pepper
1/3 cup soy sauce
60 oz or 1.8 L chicken broth, reduced-sodium
1 1/2 tsp hot chili sauce

water

2 green onions
10 oz or 300 g snow peas

7 oz or 200 g egg noodles or rice noodles

1 lb or 450 g baby carrots

<u>**Cold Veggie Dip**</u>
1/4 cup mayonnaise, light
1/4 cup sour cream, fat-free
1 tsp Mrs. Dash Original seasoning

6 multigrain dinner rolls

<u>**Serves 4-6**</u>

25 Ready, Let's Eat

Equipment List:

...the night before...
Large stove-top pot
Slow cooker
Large mixing spoon
Measuring cups and spoons

...when you get home...
Stove-top pot
Cutting board
Sharp veggie knife
Large stirring spoon
Small stirring spoon
Ladle
Measuring cups and spoons

Per serving:

Calories	507
Fat	11.6 g
Protein	39.3 g
Carbohydrate	63.3 g
Fiber	6.0 g
Sodium	970 mg

U.S. Food Exchanges:		Cdn. Food Choices:	
3 1/2	Starch	4	Carb
5	Meat-lean	5	Meat/Alt
1	Vegetable		

Prep Time

About the Recipes

Green

This recipe can be made two different ways. I either cook it on the grill or if it's a cold day, pop it in the oven and bake it at 350° F for 50 minutes.

If you are a vegetarian you can cut the sauce down and marinate tofu, or just add beans to the rice and nuts to the salad.

Blue

This meal is a hit with the kids and adults love it too.

Veggie grind is the perfect replacement for extra lean ground beef if you are vegetarian. If you are not fond of veggie grind simply saute it in a little curry powder. It doesn't taste like curry is in the dish, it just takes that veggie grind flavor away (if that makes sense).

Red

This roast is sooo good you will never make roast any other way. I cook this on days when I have no idea when I am coming home. Even though I like rare to medium rare meat, if I am away much longer the roast still tastes juicy and flavorful.

Sorry vegetarians, I can't bear to tell you to only eat fries and peas, so this is one of those few recipes you're on your own with.

Yellow

What I love about pizza is that it's fun, healthy and you can customize each pizza to everyone's liking. I remember years back Ron and I tried a veggie pizza with similar ingredients then started making it at home. We made pepperoni pizza for the kids. Now we have to make two 'cause most of the kids go for the veggie pizza first. Bye bye pepperoni!

Red Wings

This salmon is sooo delicious! I actually crave it. I originally created it for a food brochure I was working on, and it's been a family favorite ever since. If you have a child who doesn't care for salmon, make a piece of chicken for them, that way you aren't making two separate meals and everyone is happy.

If you are a fried tofu lover, you're in luck vegetarians!

Week 2

Green: Japanese Grilled Chicken, Rice and Stir-Fry Veggies

Our family rating: 9.5
Your family rating: _____

Blue: Creamy Noodle Bake with Spinach Salad

Our family rating: 10
Your family rating: _____

Red: All Day Roast with Fries and Peas

Our family rating: 10
Your family rating: _____

Yellow: Pizza and a Tossed Green Salad

Our family rating: 10
Your family rating: _____

Red Wings: Salmon with Cranberry-Lime Sauce, Rice and Broccoli

Our family rating: 9
Your family rating: _____

Japanese Grilled Chicken, Rice and Stir-Fry Veggies

Instructions:

...the night before...

Take out equipment.

1. Stir the following ingredients together using a fork, in the bottom of a 9" x 13" cake pan: egg, salt, paprika, honey, sesame oil, soy sauce and lime juice.
   Add chicken, turning with fork until well coated.

   Note; You don't have to marinade chicken the night before, but it's waaay better if you do!

...when you get home...

2. Heat **BBQ** at medium heat, approx 350° F.

3. Combine rice and water in a large microwave-safe pot with lid. **Microwave** at high for 10 minutes, then medium for 10 minutes. Let stand.

...while rice is cooking...

4. When **BBQ** is hot, place marinated chicken thighs on grill, drizzling the balance of marinade over each thigh. Cook each side approx 7 to 10 minutes, or until juices run clear and internal temperature of thighs reach 180° F.

...while chicken is cooking...

4. Wash and cut zucchini, mushrooms, red onion and red pepper into chunks.

   If you have a **BBQ** grill basket, drizzle oil and sprinkle spice on vegetable mixture before cooking.
   Toss occasionally until slightly crisp.
   ...or...
   Heat oil in a **fry pan** or wok at medium high. Add veggies, sprinkle with spice, and reduce heat to medium, tossing occasionally until slightly crisp.

Ingredients:

Take out ingredients.
1 egg
1/4 tsp salt
1 Tbsp paprika
1/4 cup honey
2 Tbsp sesame oil
2 Tbsp soy sauce, reduced-sodium
1 Tbsp lime juice

12-16 chicken thighs, boneless, skinless (1 3/4 lbs or 800 g)

1 1/2 cups basmati or jasmine rice
3 cups water

1 medium zucchini
5 mushrooms
1/4 red onion
1/2 red pepper
1 tsp olive oil
1/2 tsp Mrs. Dash Original seasoning

<u>**Serves 4-6**</u>

40 Ready, Let's Eat

Equipment List:

...the night before...
9" x 13" cake pan
Fork
Measuring cups and spoons

...when you get home...
BBQ grill basket or fry pan
Large microwave-safe pot w/lid
Cutting board
Sharp veggie knife
Flipper
Stirring spoon
Measuring cups and spoons

Per serving:

Calories	402
Fat	9.2 g
Protein	31.3 g
Carbohydrate	47.2 g
Fiber	1.9 g
Sodium	278 mg

U.S. Food Exchanges:		Cdn. Food Choices:	
3	Starch	3	Carb
3	Meat-lean	3	Meat/Alt

Data assumes half the
chicken marinade is discarded.

15

WEEK 2

Prep Time

Creamy Noodle Bake with Spinach Salad

Instructions:

Don't change yet! Take out equipment.
1. Preheat **oven** to 400° F.

2. Fill a large **stove-top** pot with water and bring to a boil for pasta.

3. Brown ground beef in a large nonstick **fry pan** at med-high. When meat is no longer pink, stir in tomato soup, spice and water.

4. Add noodles to boiling water. Set timer for 3 minutes.

5. Whisk mushroom soup and milk together, in a medium size bowl.

    When timer rings for noodles, drain in a colander, then stir noodles gently under running water to remove starch.

    Layer, in this order, in a lasagna or cake pan; 1/2 of the meat mixture, 1/2 of the cooked noodles *(you may need to run water through the noodles again to separate them before layering)*, 1/2 of the soup mixture, then the cheddar cheese.
    Repeat the same layers ending with mozzarella cheese.

    Bake in preheated **oven**, uncovered.
    Set timer for 30 minutes.
    ...meanwhile...

6. Rinse spinach leaves in basket of salad spinner. Spin dry.
    Crumble feta cheese, segment mandarins, sliver onion, and set out cashews, all in small serving dishes.

    Serve with your favorite salad dressing.

Ingredients:

Take out ingredients.
water

1 lb or 450 g extra lean ground beef
1 can tomato soup (10 oz or 284 mL)
1 tsp Italian seasoning, salt free
1/3 cup water

broad egg noodles (6 oz or 170 g)
   I like No Yolk.

1 can cream of mushroom soup
   (10 oz or 284 mL)
1/2 soup can filled with 1% milk

1/2 the meat sauce
1/2 cooked noodles
1/2 mushroom soup mixture
1/2 cup light cheddar cheese, shredded

1/2 cup part-skim mozzarella, shredded

1 bag baby spinach (12 oz or 350 g)

1/2 cup light feta cheese
3 fresh mandarins or 1 can mandarins,
   drained
1/8 of a red onion, slivered
1/2 cup cashews
1/3 cup of your favorite dressing, fat-free
   My family love strawberry vinaigrette with this meal.

<u>Serves 4-6</u>

Ready, Let's Eat

Equipment List:

Large stove-top pot
Large nonstick fry pan
Lasagna or large cake pan
Colander
Medium mixing bowl
Cutting board
Salad spinner
Grater for cheese
4 small serving bowls
Sharp veggie knife
Whisk
Can opener
Spatula
Mixing spoon
Measuring cups and spoons

Per serving:

Calories	537
Fat	18.1 g
Protein	36.1 g
Carbohydrate	59.0 g
Fiber	4.8 g
Sodium	1116 mg

U.S. Food Exchanges:		Cdn. Food Choices:	
3	Starch	3 1/2	Carb
3	Meat-lean	3	Meat/Alt
1/2	Vegetable	2	Fat
1/2	Milk-reduced fat		

20

WEEK 2

Prep Time

All Day Roast with Fries and Peas

Instructions:

...in the morning...

1. Preheat **oven** to 450° F.
    Sprinkle roast with spices and place in roasting pan, uncovered, in preheated oven. Set timer for 15 minutes.
    When timer rings **reduce heat to 180° F. DO NOT OPEN OVEN.** Leave uncovered roast in oven until you get home from work (approx 8 hours).
    Tip; If you are away longer than 8 hours, it just means that the roast will not be rare to medium rare as shown, but still tender!

    ...when you get home reset oven to 350° F...
2. Set timer for 20 minutes.

3. Rinse and place peas in a microwave-safe pot with lid. **Microwave** on high for 4 minutes, then let stand.

4. When timer rings for roast, remove from oven and wrap it in foil to rest.
    Reset oven to 450° F for the fries.

5. Place fries on a large cookie sheet and sprinkle with a little seasoning salt if you like. Place in preheated oven for 5 minutes. Flip fries and reset timer for an additional 5 minutes.

    ...meanwhile...
6. *Drain juices into a stove-top pan if you want a little gravy. Whisk gravy mix and water into juices and bring gravy to a boil, stirring continuously. Reduce heat to simmer once gravy thickens.*

7. Stir peas and reheat for 2 minutes just before serving. Add butter if you must.

Ingredients:

Note It is important roast is no less than 3 lbs or 1350 g or it will be overcooked.
lean sirloin roast or prime rib roast (3 lbs or 1350 g)
1 tsp garlic & herb seasoning, salt free
1/2 tsp garlic powder (optional)
fresh ground pepper

4 cups frozen peas

aluminum foil

1 lb or 450 g 5 minute fries
  (...which in my opinion take 10 minutes, but are amazing)
seasoning salt (optional)

Optional Gravy
3 Tbsp powdered gravy mix combined with
3 Tbsp water I like Bisto brand

butter (optional)

Serves 4-6
Use leftovers for sandwiches.

Ready, Let's Eat

Equipment List:

...in the morning...
Roasting pan
Measuring spoons

...when you get home...
Large cookie sheet
Microwave-safe pot w/lid
Stove-top pan for gravy
Cutting board for roast
Aluminum foil
Flipper
Carving knife for roast
2 mixing spoons
Fork
Measuring cups and spoons

Per serving:

Calories	437
Fat	16.9 g
Protein	39.5 g
Carbohydrate	31.8 g
Fiber	6.3 g
Sodium	194 mg

U.S. Food Exchanges:	Cdn. Food Choices:
1 1/2 Starch	1 1/2 Carb
5 Meat-lean	5 Meat/Alt
1/2 Fat	1/2 Fat

Data assumes one third
of roast is leftover.

15

Prep Time

WEEK 2

Pizza and a Tossed Green Salad

Instructions:

Don't change yet! Take out equipment.
1. **Preheat oven to 350°F.**

Vegetarian Pizza
Spread pesto all over crust. Layer over pesto in this order, as you thinly slice; zucchini, mushrooms, onion and peppers *(if someone isn't fond of something, cut large so they can pull them off easily).*
Anything else you enjoy...load it on.
Our family loves asparagus on this as well.

Scatter feta cheese then mozzarella cheese.
Top with pine nuts.

Make 2 of one kind of pizza or 1 of each.

Ham, Mushroom and Pineapple Pizza
Brush a thin layer of olive oil all over crust.
This prevents it from getting soggy.
Spread pizza sauce all over crust then layer in this order; spice, ham, mushrooms, pineapple, cheese, you name it!!!

Bake in hot **oven** on separate racks, on opposite sides of oven, for 10 minutes.
If you have a convection oven. then they just need to be on separate racks.

When timer rings, you may like to melt your cheese more by broiling one at a time until the cheese bubbles. Babysit them though as there is nothing worse than charred pizza.

2. Rinse lettuce leaves in salad spinner and spin dry. Rinse grapes.
Prepare desired toppings.

Assemble salad with your favorite toppings and dressing.

Ingredients:

Take out ingredients.

2 (12") thin crust pizza bases
Ingredients for 1 pizza
1/4 cup basil pesto (in a jar)
1/3 of a small zucchini
5 mushrooms
1/4 red onion
1/3 red pepper
1/3 orange or yellow pepper
any other veggies on hand

1/4 cup feta cheese
1 cup mozzarella cheese, part-skim, shredded
1 Tbsp pine nuts

Ingredients for 2nd pizza
1 tsp olive oil per pizza
1/2 cup pizza sauce
1 tsp Italian seasoning, salt free
deli ham, lean cooked (5 oz or 140 g)
5 mushrooms
1/2 cup pineapple tidbits, drained
1 cup mozzarella cheese, part-skim, shredded

All toppings are optional for either pizza and anything can be added.

1 head green leaf lettuce
1 cup red or black seedless grapes
slivered red onion, crumbled feta cheese, nuts, etc. (optional)
1/3 cup of your favorite dressing, fat-free
  I like creamy onion.

Serves 6-8

30 Ready, Let's Eat

Equipment List:

Salad bowl
Cutting board
Salad spinner
Flipper
Pastry brush
Can opener
Sharp veggie knife
Spreading knife
Grater for cheese
Measuring cups and spoons

Per serving:

Calories	391
Fat	16.3 g
Protein	20.3 g
Carbohydrate	43.3 g
Fiber	4.0 g
Sodium	983 mg

U.S. Food Exchanges:	Cdn. Food Choices:
2 Starch	2 1/2 Carb
2 1/2 Meat-lean	2 1/2 Meat/Alt
1 Fruit	1 1/2 Fat
1 1/2 Fat	

20

WEEK 2

Prep Time

Salmon with Cranberry-Lime Sauce, Rice and Broccoli

Instructions:

Don't change yet! Take out equipment.

1. Combine rice and water in a large microwave-safe pot with lid.
   Cover and **microwave** at high 10 minutes, then medium 10 minutes.

   …while rice is cooking…

2. Combine cranberry and lime juice in a wide bottom **stove-top** pot.
   Bring to a boil on high heat, and then **reduce heat to med-low** for a low simmer.
   When juice is reduced to half remove from heat until ready to serve, then warm it up little.

   …while sauce is reducing...

3. Spray a nonstick **fry pan** with cooking spray.
   Wash salmon under cold water, pat dry with paper towel and season one side. Cut into 4-6 equal pieces.

   Sauté, spice side down, over med-high heat until nicely seared, approx 2 minutes.
   Season top, turn and sauté other side for 2 minutes. **Reduce heat to low**, cover and let simmer for an additional 4-5 minutes then remove from heat.

   …while salmon is cooking…

4. Rinse broccoli in colander under cold water.
   Place in microwave-safe pot or casserole with lid.
   Cover and **microwave** at high for 4 minutes.
   Stir in spice.
   Add butter if you must.

   Serve sauce on plate and place salmon on top. You hope some drizzles under the rice. Yum!

Ingredients:

Take out ingredients.
1 1/2 cups basmati rice
3 cups water

Cranberry-Lime Sauce
2 cups cranberry juice
2 tsp lime juice

cooking spray I like Pam.
1 1/2 lbs or 675 g salmon filets, boneless skinless
1/4 tsp Mrs. Dash Original seasoning (per filet)

5 cups broccoli florets (1 lb or 450 g)

1/2 tsp herb seasoning, salt-free butter (optional)

Serves 4-6

25 Ready, Let's Eat

Equipment List:

Large microwave-safe pot w/lid
Med microwave-safe pot w/lid
Large nonstick fry pan w/lid
Wide bottom stove top pot
Colander
Cutting board
Paper towel
Sharp knife
Flipper
Mixing spoons
Measuring cups and spoons

Per serving:

Calories	363.5
Fat	4.9 g
Protein	28.5 g
Carbohydrate	51.6 g
Fiber	0.7 g
Sodium	100 mg

U.S. Food Exchanges:		Cdn. Food Choices:
3	Starch	3 1/2 Carb
3	Meat-very lean	2 1/2 Meat/Alt
1	Vegetable	

15

WEEK 2

Prep Time

About the Recipes

Red Wings

I don't think I have ever interviewed a family yet who didn't love tacos! These ones are easy to make and you don't need a package, just basic stuff from home.

Vegetarians, use veggie grind, but before you do, toss in a little mild curry powder (even if you don't like curry). You can't taste it, but it really makes a difference in the flavor of the tacos.

Green

Mac and cheese with a healthy twist. Parents if you want the kids to help out, this is a good one to get them started on. Simply cook the pasta the night before and toss in a little olive oil so it doesn't glob together. The kids can assemble the meal after school. Now that's cool! If you are a vegetarian that doesn't eat fish take it out and up the cheese a little.

Red

There was a dad, who loved to cook, on my show but rarely did because of his schedule. The family loved his famous ribs. You can imagine how my crew howled when I discovered his famous rib spice consisted of salt and pepper. We ribbed him about that all weekend. Vegetarians, add 1/2 a can mixed beans, 1/4 cup raisins and 1/4 cup salsa to the couscous. This packs it with the nutrition you need and as a bonus; it turns into a great cold salad for work the next day!

Yellow

This meal is so easy and a real treat! I love experimenting with weird stuff, like pie filling. Minced meat is a great flavor boost in many Indian and African dishes and is perfect in this one.

Vegetarians can take out the chicken and add tofu.

Blue

Vegetarians, when serving steak, I always suggest grilling a portabella mushroom. I load on pineapple, zucchini, sundried tomatoes, gruyere cheese and pine nuts. Wrap it in foil for about 5 minutes to soften it up, then put it directly on the grill to add that smoked flavor.

Week 3

Red Wings: Soft or Hard Shell Tacos with Toppings

Our family rating: 9.5
Your family rating: _____

Green: Tuna Tetrazzini with Corn and Peas

Our family rating: 8
Your family rating: _____

Red: Dry Ribs with Couscous and Broccoli

Our family rating: 8.5
Your family rating: _____

Yellow: Sweet Indian Chicken with Rice
and Spinach Salad

Our family rating: 9.5
Your family rating: _____

Blue: Chipotle Steak with Balsamic Reduction,
Baby Potatoes and Italian Veggies

Our family rating: 9
Your family rating: _____

3

Soft or Hard Shell Tacos with Toppings

Instructions:	Ingredients:
Don't change yet! Take out equipment.	Take out ingredients.

Instructions:

Don't change yet! Take out equipment.

1. Brown ground beef in large nonstick **fry pan** at med-high until no longer pink.
   Add spices while meat is browning, stirring occasionally.

   Add ketchup and water after meat has browned.
   Reduce heat to simmer.
   Meat mixture will thicken within 10 minutes.

   ...meanwhile...

2. Chop green onion and cilantro and slice tomatoes.

   Rinse lettuce in a salad spinner and spin dry.

   Set out toppings into small serving bowls on dinner table.

4. Spoon meat mixture into tortilla and sprinkle with cheese.
   Add your favorite toppings.
   Roll up your tortilla folding the bottom up to prevent leaking.

   This is such a fun and easy meal!

Ingredients:

Take out ingredients.
1 lb or 450 g ground beef, extra lean

2 tsp chili powder
2 tsp onion flakes
1 tsp cumin powder
1/4 tsp turmeric

1/2 cup ketchup
1/2 cup water

Toppings
4 green onions
1/2 cup cilantro
4 Roma tomatoes
1 head leaf lettuce

1/2 cup sour cream, fat-free
1/2 cup chunky salsa
3/4 cup Cheddar cheese, light, shredded

6-10 soft tortillas, 10"
hard shell tacos (optional)

Serves 4-6

25 Ready, Let's Eat

Equipment List:

Large nonstick fry pan
Cutting board
Salad spinner
Cheese grater
4-6 small serving bowls
Sharp veggie knife
Mixing spoon
Measuring cups and spoons

Per serving:

Calories	416
Fat	10.9 g
Protein	28.7 g
Carbohydrate	50.8 g
Fiber	4.4 g
Sodium	972 mg

U.S. Food Exchanges:		Cdn. Food Choices:	
3	Starch	3	Carb
3	Meat-lean	3	Meat/Alt

15

Prep Time

WEEK 3

Tuna Tetrazzini with Corn and Peas

Instructions:

Don't change yet! Take out equipment.

1. Fill a large **stove-top** pot with water and bring to a boil on high heat.

2. Preheat **oven** to 350° F.

   Heat oil in a large nonstick **fry pan** at med-high heat. Finely chop onion and slice celery adding to pan as you cut. Sauté until onion is soft and slightly browned.

3. Add pasta to boiling water. Set timer according to package directions (approx 10 minutes).

4. Add mushroom soup to sauteed onion and gradually stir in milk until all ingredients are combined. **Remove from heat.**

5. When timer rings for pasta, rinse in a colander with cold water to remove starch.

6. Layer ingredients into a large oven-proof casserole starting with pasta then cheese. Drain tuna and crumble evenly all over layer of cheese. Pour sauce evenly all over, then the final layer of cheese. Cover tightly with foil and place in hot **oven**. Set timer for 25 minutes.

7. Rinse peas and corn in a colander. Place in a microwave-safe pot or casserole with lid. **Microwave** at high for 4 minutes. Add butter if you must and stir.

8. When timer rings for casserole, **broil** top for 2 additional minutes, but watch carefully *(or even better...set the timer for a minute so you don't get distracted and the next thing you know you have a very black casserole! Think I've been there?)*

Ingredients:

Take out ingredients.
water

1 tsp olive oil
1/2 onion
1 celery stalk

4 cups cavatappi pasta
 (any kind of spiral pasta will do)

1 can cream of mushroom soup
 (10 oz or 284 mL)
1/2 of the soup can, filled with 1% milk

cooked pasta
1/2 cup Tex-Mex cheese, shredded
1 can solid tuna in water, drained
 (6 1/2 oz or 180 g)
mushroom sauce
1 cup Tex-Mex cheese, shredded
aluminum foil

2 cups frozen peas
2 cups frozen corn
1 tsp butter (optional)

<u>**Serves 4-6**</u>

45 Ready, Let's Eat

Equipment List:

Large nonstick fry pan
Large stove-top pot
Large casserole dish w/lid
Microwave-safe pot w/lid
Cutting board
Colander
Can opener
Sharp veggie knife
Mixing spoon
Measuring cups and spoons
Aluminum foil

Per serving:

Calories	410
Fat	12.9 g
Protein	23.0 g
Carbohydrate	52.2 g
Fiber	4.5 g
Sodium	833 mg

U.S. Food Exchanges:		Cdn. Food Choices:	
3	Starch	3	Carb
2 1/2	Meat-lean	2 1/2	Meat/Alt
1/2	Vegetable	1	Fat
1	Fat		

15

Prep Time

Dry Ribs with Couscous and Broccoli

Instructions:

...the night before...

Take out equipment.

1. Place ribs on broiler pan and sprinkle with salt and pepper.

...or...

Mix together ingredients for the optional rub mixture and rub onto both sides of ribs.

...in the morning...

2. **Preheat oven to 400° F.**
   Place ribs in preheated **oven** for 5 minutes. Turn and cook 5 more minutes. **Reduce heat** to 175° F. Cover ribs with foil and leave in oven all day **approx 8-10 hrs**.

...just before dinner...

3. Heat oil in a small **stove-top** pot at medium. Finely chop onion adding to pot as you cut. Add garlic and stir.
   Wash and slice mushrooms adding to pot as you cut. Cook until soft.
   Add water and chicken broth to pot and bring to a boil. Add couscous to pot and stir. **Remove from heat.** Cover and let stand 5 minutes. Just before serving chop tomato and cilantro and stir into couscous.

4. Rinse broccoli in a colander.
   Place in a microwave-safe pot or casserole. Cover and **microwave** at high 4 minutes. Toss with butter if you must.

This simple little hands free task the night before makes a week day meal, special!

Ingredients:

Take out ingredients.
2 1/2 lbs or 1125 g lean pork or beef ribs
1/2 tsp salt
1/2 tsp freshly ground pepper

<u>Optional Rub Mixture</u>
2 Tbsp brown sugar
2 Tbsp paprika
1 tsp dry mustard
1 tsp garlic & herb seasoning, salt free
1/2 tsp freshly ground pepper

aluminum foil

1 tsp olive oil
1/2 small onion
1 tsp fresh garlic (from a jar)
6 mushrooms
1 cup water
1 cup chicken broth, reduced-sodium
1 cup couscous

1 Roma tomato
1/4 cup cilantro

1 lb or 450 g broccoli florets

1 tsp butter (optional)

<u>Serves 4-6</u>

Ready, Let's Eat

Equipment List:

...on the weekend...
Broiler pan
Aluminum foil
Plastic wrap
Measuring spoons
...just before dinner...
Broiler pan
Small stove-top pot
Microwave-safe pot w/lid
Cutting board
Colander
Can opener
Sharp veggie knife
Mixing spoon
Fork or tongs
Measuring cups and spoons

Per serving:

Calories	494
Fat	28.5 g
Protein	29.6 g
Carbohydrate	29.8 g
Fiber	2.2 g
Sodium	323 mg

U.S. Food Exchanges:		Cdn. Food Choices:	
2	Starch	2	Carb
3	Meat-high fat	3	Meat/Alt
1	Fat	4	Fat

Prep Time

15

WEEK 3

Sweet Indian Chicken with Rice and Spinach Salad

Instructions:

Don't change yet! Take out equipment.

1. Toss cloves into the bottom of a medium size **stove-top** pot at med-high. When cloves become fragrant, add butter and rice. Stir. Add water. Cover pot and bring to a boil. **Reduce heat** and simmer. Set timer for 20 minutes, lifting rice once with a fork half way through cooking.
   ...meanwhile...

2. Heat oil in a large nonstick **fry pan** at med-high heat.
   Cut chicken into bite-size pieces adding to pan as you cut. Toss until no longer pink.

   Finely chop onion adding to pan as you chop. Add garlic and ginger. Stir to combine flavors and let cook an extra minute.

   Add chicken broth, curry paste and mincemeat to pan.

   Bring to a boil then **reduce heat** to simmer.
   ...meanwhile...
   Smash peanuts in a clean folded dish towel with a hammer.
   Rinse and chop cilantro.
   Place in small serving bowls.

3. Rinse spinach in basket of salad spinner and spin dry.
   Toss salad with your favorite salad dressing and toppings.

   Serve chicken over rice in bowls, along with mango chutney if you wish.
   Garnish with smashed peanuts and chopped cilantro. Sooooo good!

Ingredients:

Take out ingredients.
4-5 whole dry cloves

1 tsp butter
1 1/2 cups basmati rice
3 cups water

1 tsp canola or olive oil

4 boneless skinless chicken breasts, or chicken tenders (1 1/3 lb or 600 g)

1 onion
2 tsp fresh garlic (from a jar)
  or 2 cloves finely chopped
2 tsp fresh ginger (from a jar)
  or fresh grated ginger root

2 cups chicken broth, reduced-sodium
3 tsp Madras curry paste
1/2 cup mincemeat
  (in a jar, found with dessert pie fillings)

1/2 cup Spanish peanuts (optional)

1/2 cup fresh cilantro

1 bag spinach leaves (12 oz or 350 g)

1/3 cup of your favorite dressing, fat-free
Optional Toppings
  mandarin segments, slivered red onion, nuts, etc.
mango chutney (optional)

30 Ready, Let's Eat

<u>Serves 4-6</u>

Equipment List:

Medium stove-top pot w/lid
Large nonstick fry pan
2 cutting boards
Salad spinner
Salad bowl
2 small serving bowls
Can opener
Sharp meat knife
Sharp veggie knife
Mixing spoon
Fork
Measuring cups and spoons
Hammer
Clean dish towel

Per serving:

Calories	412
Fat	5.5 g
Protein	30.8 g
Carbohydrate	58.5 g
Fiber	2.8 g
Sodium	372 mg

U.S. Food Exchanges:		Cdn. Food Choices:	
3	Starch	3 1/2 Carb	
3	Meat-lean	3	Meat/Alt
2	Vegetable		

20

Prep Time

WEEK 3

Chipotle Steak with Balsamic Reduction, Baby Potatoes and Italian Veggies

Instructions:

Don't change yet! Take out equipment.

1. Wash and slice celery, pepper and cucumber. Place in a medium size bowl as you cut.

   Rinse baby carrots in a colander. Add carrots and tomatoes to bowl.

   Toss with olive oil, balsamic vinegar and spice. Let stand.

2. Wash potatoes and place in a large **stove-top** pot of cold water. Bring to boil at high, uncovered, then **reduce heat** to medium. Cook until potatoes are easily pierced with a fork. (approx 10 minutes)

3. Heat oil in a small **stove-top** pot at medium. Finely chop onion. adding to pot as you cut. Sauté slightly then add garlic and ginger.

   Continue stirring for a minute then add balsamic vinegar, maple syrup and wine. Simmer until mixture reduces to half. **Remove from heat.**

   ...just before dinner...

4. Preheat **BBQ or broiler**. Sprinkle spice all over steak.

   Grill steak to your preferred doneness and then rest in foil.

   Just before steaks are done reheat balsamic reduction. When hot, pool sauce on each plate then place steak on top of the sauce. Serve potatoes and veggies along side.

Ingredients:

Take out ingredients.
2 celery stalks
1/2 red pepper
1/2 English cucumber
1 cup washed baby carrots
1 cup cherry tomatoes

1 Tbsp olive oil
1 Tbsp balsamic vinegar
1 tsp Italian seasoning

20 baby potatoes or cut up 4 large

Balsamic Reduction for Steak
1 tsp olive oil
2 Tbsp red onion
2 tsp fresh garlic
  (from a jar or chop 2 large cloves)
1/2 tsp grated fresh ginger (or from a jar)

1/4 cup balsamic vinegar
2 Tbsp maple syrup
1/4 cup white wine
  or reduced-sodium beef broth

1 Tbsp chipotle seasoning, salt free
1 1/2 lbs or 675 g very thick top sirloin
  steak, boneless and trimmed
aluminum foil

Serves 4-6

35 Ready, Let's Eat

Equipment List:

BBQ or broiler pan
BBQ tongs
Large stove-top pot
Small stove-top pot
Cutting board
Colander
Medium serving bowl
Sharp veggie knife
2 mixing spoons
Fork
Measuring cups and spoons
Aluminum foil

Per serving:

Calories	328
Fat	7.8 g
Protein	26.5 g
Carbohydrate	39.0 g
Fiber	4.9 g
Sodium	94 mg

U.S. Food Exchanges:		Cdn. Food Choices:	
2	Starch	2 1/2 Carb	
3	Meat-lean	3	Meat/Alt
1	Vegetable		

20

Prep Time

WEEK 3

About the Recipes

Green

This takes meatloaf to the next millenium! Our eating is so cross cultural now a days, thank goodness for that. By forming the meatloaf on a broiler pan, all the oil drips to the catch pan underneath. The spices on the inside of the meatloaf and the chutney on the outside form a perfect union of flavors.
Vegetarians you are on your own tonight!

Red Wings

This meal is so fun. It's often a movie night meal for our family. It's kinda cool when the kids think you are eating junk food and you're not. It also suits the sophisticated palette of adults.
Vegetarians, this is an easy one, soak some tofu in the dressing first, then make the wraps with all the veggies you like. Nuts are great too!

Yellow

I love putting bolognaise sauce in the crock pot 'cause there is nothing like a sauce that has simmered a looong time. The first time we made squash for this sauce we cooked pasta as well, just in case the kids didn't like it. Some looove it, and some don't! It's my favorite now!
If you are vegetarian, veggie grind works great!

Blue

We hear about beer can chicken, but we like ours with ginger ale. This chicken is sooo tender and delicious! It does need a little babysitting, but man, it's worth it.
Sorry vegetarians, other than BBQing a good veggie burger, I can't help you on this one! Mind you, the reduction is so yummy, hum, veggie burger...not a bad idea!

Red Wings

This is such a great meal, both easy to make for the family or for entertaining.
If you are vegetarian, but don't eat fish, replace shrimp with fried tofu.

Week 4

4

Green: Chutney Glazed Meatloaf,
Baby Potatoes and Broccoli

> Our family rating: 9
> Your family rating: _____

Red Wings: Thai Chicken Wraps

> Our family rating: 10
> Your family rating: _____

Yellow: Crock-Pot Bolognaise on Spaghetti Squash
and Peas

> Our family rating: 10
> Your family rating: _____

Blue: Ginger Ale Chicken with Foccacia
and Green Leaf Salad

> Our family rating: 9.5
> Your family rating: _____

Red Wings: Seafood Curry on Penne Pasta
with Green Beans

> Our family rating: 8
> Your family rating: _____

Chutney Glazed Meatloaf, Baby Potatoes and Broccoli

Instructions:

Don't change yet! Take out equipment.

1. Preheat **oven** to 350°F.
    Combine the following in a large bowl:
    ground beef, salt, pepper, egg, breadcrumbs,
    garlic, garam masala and curry paste. Mix
    well. (I use my hands).

    Form meat into a long flat loaf shape on top of
    a broiler pan.

    Combine plum sauce, peach jam and curry
    powder in the uncleaned bowl.

    Spread over top of meatloaf.
    Place loaf in hot **oven**. Set timer for 30
    minutes (total bake time is 50 minutes).

2. When timer rings for meatloaf, leave it in.

    Wash potatoes and place in a large stove-top
    pot filled with cold water. Bring to a boil then
    reduce heat to a low boil. Cook until tender
    (about 10 minutes).

    ..meanwhile...

3. Rinse broccoli in a colander. Place in a
    microwave-safe pot with lid. **Microwave** at
    high 4 minutes. Toss with butter if you must.

4. Drain potatoes and return to pot. Add a little
    butter and toss the potatoes to coat. Cover to
    keep warm until dinner is all ready!

    *Meatloaf is ready when instant read
    thermometer reaches 180°F.*

Ingredients:

Take out ingredients.

2 lbs or 900 g extra lean ground beef
pinch salt
1/4 tsp fresh pepper
1 egg
1/2 cup fine breadcrumbs
2 tsp fresh garlic (from a jar)
2 tsp garam masala
  (can be hard to find but worth it)
  See page 32-33 for a description.
2 Tbsp Tandoori curry paste

Plum Peach Chutney Glaze
2 Tbsp plum sauce
2 Tbsp peach jam
1/4 tsp curry powder

20 baby potatoes or cut up 4 large

1 lb or 450 g broccoli florets

butter (optional)

1 tsp butter

Serves 4-6

60 Ready, Let's Eat

Equipment List:

Broiler pan
Large stove-top pot
Microwave-safe pot w/lid
Cutting board
Large bowl
Small bowl
Colander
Sharp veggie knife
Mixing spoon
Measuring cups and spoons

Per serving:

Calories	420
Fat	9.5 g
Protein	37.3 g
Carbohydrate	46.2 g
Fiber	4.4 g
Sodium	455 mg

U.S. Food Exchanges:		Cdn. Food Choices:	
2	Starch	2 1/2	Carb
4	Meat-lean	4	Meat/Alt
2	Vegetable		

15

WEEK 4

Prep Time

Thai Chicken Wraps

Instructions:

Don't change yet! Take out equipment.

1. Fill a **kettle** with water and bring to a boil.

2. Heat oil in a large nonstick **fry pan** at medium heat. Cut chicken into small bite size pieces adding to pan as you cut. Stir until meat is no longer pink.
Cover and remove from heat.

3. Place noodles in a casserole dish and completely cover with boiling water.
Set timer according to package insructions (about 3-5 minutes)
When timer rings for noodles, drain in a colander and set aside.

   ....meanwhile...
4. **Microwave** peanut butter for 7 seconds in a microwave-safe bowl. Whisk in Catalina dressing, garlic, lime juice, Chinese cooking wine, soy sauce, ginger powder and sweet chili sauce. Set aside.

5. Rinse lettuce in basket of salad spinner, spin dry. Peel carrots and cut into tiny long narrow sticks (julienne).
Wash cucumber and do the same.
Wash and sliver red pepper.
Rinse bean sprouts.

6. Give noodles a rinse separating gently with your fingers.

   Lay tortillas on plate. Layer with lettuce and cooked noodles.
Add chicken, then drizzle with dressing.
Top with cut carrots, cucumber, red pepper and bean sprouts. Fantastic!

Ingredients:

Take out ingredients.
water

1 tsp sesame oil
3 chicken breasts, boneless, skinless
 (1 lb or 450 g)

1/4 lb or 113 g rice stick noodles

Thai Wrap Sauce
1/4 cup peanut butter, light
1/2 cup Catalina salad dressing, low-fat
1 tsp fresh garlic (frm a jar)
1 Tbsp lime juice
1 Tbsp Chinese cooking wine, nonalcoholic
2 tsp soy sauce, reduced-sodium
1 tsp ginger powder
1 Tbsp sweet chili sauce

1 head green leaf lettuce or bagged lettuce
2 large carrots (or now you can find these
 already cut julienne style!)
1/2 English cucumber
1 red pepper
1/2 lb or 225 g bean sprouts (optional)

6-10 whole wheat or corn tortillas, 10"

25 Ready, Let's Eat

<u>Serves 4-6</u>

Equipment List:

Large nonstick fry pan
Casserole dish
Microwave-safe bowl
2 cutting boards
Kettle
Salad spinner
Colander
Sharp meat knife
Sharp veggie knife
Peeler for carrots
Whisk
Mixing spoons
Measuring cups and spoons

Per serving:

Calories	490
Fat	11.5 g
Protein	28.3 g
Carbohydrate	69.2 g
Fiber	5.4 g
Sodium	919 mg

U.S. Food Exchanges:		Cdn. Food Choices:	
3 1/2	Starch	4	Carb
2	Meat-lean	2	Meat/Alt
2	Vegetable	1	Fat
1	Fat		

15

Prep Time

Crock-Pot Bolognaise on Spaghetti Squash and Peas

Instructions:

…the night before…
Take out equipment.

1. Heat oil in a lge nonstick **fry pan** at med-high. Chop onion and shallot adding to pan as you cut. Sauté until slightly browned. Add garlic and beef. Cook until beef is no longer pink. Toss everything into **crock of slowcooker**.

   Finely chop green pepper and slice mushrooms, adding to pot as you cut. Add sauce, tomatoes and tomato paste. Stir, cover and place in **fridge** overnight.

…in the morning...

2. Return crock with lid to the **slow cooker** and set on low heat.

…when you get home…

3. Wash the outside of spaghetti squash and place in microwave at high for 7 minutes.

…while squash is cooking…

4. Rinse peas in a colander and place in a microwave-safe pot with lid. When timer rings for squash take it out of the microwave and submerge in a bowl of cold water. *This will make it easier to cut.*
   Microwave peas at high for 4 minutes.

5. Once squash is cool enough to handle, cut in half lengthwise. Scrape the seeds out, brush olive oil on the inside of both halves. Sprinkle with curry powder and place in a microwave safe pan flesh side down.(they can be stacked)
   ...when timer rings for peas...
   Take them out and put squash in. Set timer for 8 minutes. Once cooked, Scrape the flesh with a fork lengthwise to create long spaghetti like strands.
   Serve the sauce over top like you would if you cooked pasta. Our family loves hot chili flakes and Parmesan on top.

Ingredients:

Take out ingredients.
1 tsp olive oil
1 onion
1 shallot
2 tsp fresh garlic (from a jar)
1 lb or 450 g extra lean ground beef

1/2 green pepper (or 1 small)
10 brown or white mushrooms
1 can pasta sauce (24 oz or 680 mL)
1 can spicy pasta sauce (24 oz or 680 mL)
1 can diced tomatoes (14 oz or 398 mL)
1 can tomato paste (5 1/2 oz or 156 mL)

1 spaghetti squash (3 lbs or 1350 g)
Option: Cook spaghetti instead of the squash if you want this meal the traditional way.

4 cups frozen baby peas

1 tsp olive oil
1 tsp mild curry powder

Parmesan cheese, grated, light (optional)
red pepper flakes (optional)

I think it looks amazing when you serve this meal in the shell. A family can put the sauce in one half and squash in the other half. For a romantic dinner for two, use the shells as a plate!

Serves 6-8

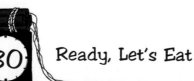

30 Ready, Let's Eat

Equipment List:

...the night before...
Crock-pot
Large nonstick fry-pan
Cutting board
Sharp veggie knife
Mixing spoon and Can opener
Measuring spoons
...when you get home...
Microwave-safe pot w/ld
Large bowl
Colander
Cutting board
Pastry brush
Sharp veggie knife
Mixing spoon and Fork
Measuring cups and spoons

Per serving:

Calories	397
Fat	9.6 g
Protein	22.8 g
Carbohydrate	58.9 g
Fiber	5.8 g
Sodium	1053 mg

U.S. Food Exchanges:		Cdn. Food Choices:	
2 1/2	Starch	3 1/2	Carb
2	Meat-lean	2 1/2	Meat/Alt
3	Vegetable	1/2	Fat
1/2	Fat		

Prep Time

Ginger Ale Chicken with Foccacia and Green Leaf Salad

Instructions:

...the night before...
Take out equipment.
1. Combine brown sugar and spices in a small bowl for rub.
   Using smoked paprika can replace wood chips for smoking. It has a similar effect, if not better.

   Wash chicken inside and out.
   Pat dry with paper towels.
   Use 1 Tbsp of the rub mixture to smear on the inside cavity of bird. Rub the remainder on the outside of the bird.

   Cover tips of legs and wings with foil.
   Place chicken in a large bowl, cover and store in **fridge** overnight.

...when you get home...
2. Preheat **BBQ** to 350° F (burners on low-med). Wash outside of soda can, open and pour out half. Puncture two more holes on the top with a can opener.

   Shove the bird over the top of the can, (*there's really no other way to say it*) making a tripod with the two front legs and the can so the bird is standing upright. Transfer to grill. Turn off the flame directly under the bird and close lid. *Chicken is ready when a meat thermometer reads 180° F in the thickest part of the thigh. (approx 55 minutes, but longer if larger bird)*
...when chicken is almost ready...
3. Place foccacia on **grill** until lightly browned. Remove and serve with oil and vinegar.

4. Rinse then spin lettuce in a salad spinner. Slice carrots and celery and add to lettuce. Rinse cherry tomatoes and add to lettuce. Serve with your favorite salad dressing.

Ingredients:

Take out ingredients.
<u>Spice Rub for Chicken</u>
1 Tbsp brown sugar
2 tsp coarse salt
2 tsp smoked paprika (or hot paprika)
1 tsp garlic powder
1/2 tsp black pepper
1/2 tsp cumin
1/4 tsp cayenne Only if you looove spicy!
1 whole roasting chicken, raw
  (3 lbs or 1350 g)
paper towels

aluminum foil

1/2 can ginger ale (use 6 oz or 175 mL)
  or use beer
Use the old fashioned puncture
  style can opener if you have one.

Note: You may have to remove the BBQ's upper rack and check barbecue occasionally for flare ups. Transfer bird from the grill to a baking pan using strong tongs and be careful of the scalding can.

1 loaf foccacia bread (1 lb or 450 g)
olive oil and balsamic vinegar (optional)

1 head green leaf lettuce
2 large carrots
2 stalks celery
12 cherry tomatoes
1/3 cup of your favorite dressing, fat-free

<u>**Serves 4-6**</u>

60 Ready, Let's Eat

Equipment List:

…the night before…
Large mixing bowl for chicken
Small bowl for spice rub
Dessert spoon for mixing
Measuring spoons
Paper towels
Aluminum foil
…when you get home…
BBQ
Salad spinner
Cutting board
Sharp veggie knife
Can opener
Meat thermometer

Per serving:

Calories	542
Fat	15.9 g
Protein	33.2 g
Carbohydrate	64.5 g
Fiber	4.5 g
Sodium	1027 mg

U.S. Food Exchanges:		Cdn. Food Choices:	
3 1/2	Starch	4	Carb
4	Meat-lean	3	Meat/Alt
1	Vegetable	1	Fat
1	Fat		

20 Prep Time

Seafood Curry on Penne Pasta with Green Beans

Instructions:

Don't change yet! Take out equipment.

1. Fill a large **stove-top** pot with water and bring to a boil.

2. Heat oil in a large nonstick **fry pan** or wok. Sliver onion adding to pan as you cut. Add sun dried tomatoes and curry powder.

   Cut mushrooms in half adding to pan as you cut. Add scallops and sauté for 2 minutes. Add pineapple juice. Gradually add mushroom soup to pan then gradually stir in milk until combined. **Reduce heat** to simmer.

3. Place pasta in boiling water. Set timer for 8-10 minutes or until al dente. *Follow your specific package directions.*

4. Heat oil in a different nonstick **fry pan**. Rinse green beans in colander and add to pan. Sprinkle with lemon pepper and soy sauce. Toss until hot, tender and glazed.

5. Fold shrimp into pasta sauce and heat through.

6. **Microwave** pineapple to warm, just before serving.

   Drain pasta and toss in a small amount of olive oil if you wish.

   On each plate place noodles, then pineapple, then sauce. (This makes it easy for those who don't care for pineapple. Just leave it out!) A sprinkle of Parmesan and cilantro adds a nice touch, especially when entertaining.

Ingredients:

Take out ingredients.

water

1 tsp canola oil
1/2 onion
3 Tbsp sun dried tomatoes in oil, drained
  (from a jar)
1 tsp mild curry powder

6 mushrooms
5 oz or 150 g scallops, fresh or frozen
1/2 cup pineapple juice
  (from the can of pineapple tidbits)
1 can cream of mushroom soup
  (10 oz or 284 mL)
2/3 of the soup can, filled with 1% milk

12 oz or 350 g baby penne pasta

1 tsp canola oil
4-5 cups frozen green beans
  (1 lb or 450 g)
1/2 tsp lemon pepper
1 Tbsp soy sauce, reduced-sodium

7 oz or 200 g deveined cooked shrimp,
  tail on

1 can pineapple tidbits
  (14 oz or 398 mL)

olive oil (optional)

Parmesan cheese, grated, light (optional)
cilantro (optional)

<u>**Serves 4-6**</u>

25 Ready, Let's Eat

Equipment List:

Large stove-top pot
2 large nonstick fry pans
  or woks
Cutting board
Small microwave-safe bowl
Colander
Can opener
Sharp veggie knife
2 mixing spoons
Measuring cups and spoons

Per serving:

Calories	415
Fat	6.3 g
Protein	22.8 g
Carbohydrate	67.3 g
Fiber	5.7 g
Sodium	578 mg

U.S. Food Exchanges:		Cdn. Food Choices:	
3	Starch	4	Carb
2	Meat-lean	2	Meat/Alt
1	Fruit		

About the Recipes

Green

Baked ham in the work week is possible as long as you are willing to boil a few potatoes the night before. Not only do you end up with a great down home dinner, but lunch meat for the week too!
Vegetarians, this sauce is really amazing, so I would go ahead and make this meal with veggie ham.

Blue

This recipe may not look great, but man is it good! This was one of our top 10 rated recipes amongst our test families. Our family doesn't pull out the tortillas until movie night to have with salsa and the left over sauce. YUM!!!
Vegetarians, make this by using mixed beans and veggies on the bottom layer.

Yellow

This doesn't taste like your average one pan meal. Aaand if you're wondering why I always put optional beside cilantro (also known as fresh coriander or Chinese parsley) it's because cilantro is just one of those things you either love or hate. Ron and I used to hate it but we're both addicted to it now!
Vegetarians, veggie grind is great in this dish!

Red

This simple Tandoori chicken is a hit with both adults and kids. I am a mango chutney freak so I like to have a little of that on the side.
Vegetarians, marinate a portabella mushroom in a fraction of the sauce and grill it up. Load it with veggies, nuts and your choice of cheese.

Yellow

No doubt, this is one of my personal favorites! I remember being intimidated at first by the whole "salmon on a plank" thing. One day, I filtered through a bunch of books, then gave it a go. I hope you find this one is the best you've ever tried.
If you are vegetarian and don't eat fish, I feel sorry for you!

Week 5

5

Green: Baked Ham with Apricot Sauce,
                Smashed Potatoes and Broccoli

                  Our family rating: 9.5
                  Your family rating: _____

Blue: Tex-Mex Chicken with Corn Muffins
                and Salad

                  Our family rating: 9
                  Your family rating: _____

Yellow: Ginger Beef with Egg Noodles
                and Snap Peas

                  Our family rating: 10
                  Your family rating: _____

Red: Tandoori Chicken with Basmati Rice
                and Peas

                  Our family rating: 9.5
                  Your family rating: _____

Yellow: BBQ Salmon on a Plank,
                Fruit Salsa and Pita Chips

                  Our family rating: 9
                  Your family rating: _____

Baked Ham with Apricot Sauce, Smashed Potatoes and Broccoli

Instructions:

...the night before...
Take out equipment.

1. Fill a large **stove-top** pot with cold water. Wash potatoes then cut into quarters, adding to pot as you cut. Bring to a boil then **reduce heat** to a low boil. Set timer for 15 minutes or until you can easily slide a knife into the potato. Drain, let cool and **refrigerate**.

...when you get home...
2. Preheat **oven** to 350° F.
Place ham in a roasting pan and pour ginger ale all over. Cover with foil and set timer for 45 minutes.

...meanwhile...
3. Rinse broccoli in colander.
Place in microwave-safe pot. Cover and **microwave** at high 4 minutes.

4. Cut apricots into small pieces and simmer in apple juice in a small **stove-top** saucepan at medium heat. Set timer for 10 minutes. Blend together brown sugar, cornstarch and spices, in a small bowl. Whisk gradually into apple juice mixture until smooth. Bring to a gentle boil. Add butter, stir, **remove from heat** and set aside.

...when timer rings for ham...
5. Baste top of ham with liquid in roasting pan. **Reset oven** to 375° F and return ham to oven. Set timer for 10 minutes. Discard liquid when done.

6. **Microwave** potatoes until hot (approx 3-4 minutes). Add garlic and butter and mash until smooth, gradually adding a little milk until firm but fluffy.
You may need a tiny bit more milk, but remember to add a drizzle at a time.

Ingredients:

Take out ingredients.
water
4 large thin skinned potatoes
  (2 lbs or 900 g)

ready-to-serve ham boneless
(3-4 lbs or 1.3-1.8 kg) reduced-sodium
1 can (12 oz or 355 mL) ginger ale
aluminum foil

5 cups broccoli florets
  (1 lb or 450 g)

Apricot Sauce
1/4 cup dried apricots
1 1/2 cups apple juice

2 Tbsp brown sugar
1 Tbsp cornstarch
pinch (1/8 tsp) ground cinnamon
pinch (1/8 tsp) ground cloves
1 Tbsp butter

previously cooked potatoes
1 tsp fresh garlic (from a jar)
2 tsp butter
1/4 cup 1% milk

Serves 4-6
Half the ham is reserved for sandwiches.

60 Ready, Let's Eat

Equipment List:

...the night before...
Large stove-top pot
Sharp knife
Cutting board
...when you get home...
Large roasting pan
Microwave-safe pot
Small stove-top saucepan
Cutting board
Small bowl
Colander
Sharp knife
Whisk and Masher
Baster and Mixing spoon
Measuring cups and spoons
Aluminum foil

Per serving:

Calories	435
Fat	9.9 g
Protein	30.2 g
Carbohydrate	58.4 g
Fiber	3.0 g
Sodium	1160 mg

U.S. Food Exchanges:	Cdn. Food Choices:
3 Starch	3 1/2 Carb
3 Meat-lean	3 Meat/Alt
1/2 Fruit	

Assumes half the ham is leftover.

WEEK 5

Prep Time

Tex-Mex Chicken with Corn Muffins and Salad

Instructions:

Don't change yet! Take out equipment.

1. Preheat **oven** to 350º F.
   Whip butter by hand or with electric beaters and gradually add eggs.
   Pour flour, baking soda, baking powder and cornmeal onto a piece of waxed paper and combine with a fork.
   Gradually blend dry mixture into the butter and eggs, alternating with the sour cream, until completely blended.
   Stir in cheddar.
   I add finely chopped jalapeños and red pepper.

   Spray muffin tins and fill 2/3 full with batter. Top with a little cheddar. Place in hot **oven** on top rack, left hand side. Set timer for 25 minutes.
   …meanwhile…

2. Cut chicken breasts in half and place chicken in a large oven proof pan. Sprinkle with spice and onion flakes. Layer cream corn, rinsed corn, pasta sauce and salsa over top in that order. Top with cheese. Place in hot **oven**, uncovered, on bottom rack, right hand side.
   Don't forget to take a look at the remaining time left for muffins when chicken goes in so you can reset the timer when you take the muffins out. The chicken needs to cook for 45 minutes.

3. Put tortilla chips in a bowl for dipping in the sauce, if you like, or save leftover sauce for a movie night.
   When the timer rings for muffins, remove from oven and let cool on a cooling rack.
   Don't forget to reset timer for chicken.

4. Rinse spinach in salad spinner and spin dry. Segment mandarin oranges. Sliver red onion and crumble feta. When timer rings for chicken, assemble salad with your favorite toppings and dressing. *We also love cashews.*

Ingredients:

Take out ingredients.
<u>Corn Muffins</u>
1/2 cup butter (softened)
2 eggs
1 cup flour
1/2 tsp baking soda
1 tsp baking powder
1/2 cup cornmeal
3/4 cup sour cream, fat-free

1/2 cup sharp or old cheddar cheese, light, shredded
1 Tbsp jalapeños and/or 1 Tbsp red pepper (optional)
cooking spray I like Pam.
1/4 cup sharp or old cheddar cheese, light, shredded

5 chicken breasts, boneless, skinless or thighs (**1 2/3 lbs or 750 g**)
2 tsp chipotle seasoning, salt free or chili powder
1 tsp oregano leaves
1 Tbsp onion flakes
1 cup creamed corn
1/2 cup frozen corn
1 1/2 cups tomato sauce I like Hunts Italian
1/2 cup salsa
1 cup Tex-Mex cheese, shredded, light

tortilla chips (optional)

1 bag prewashed spinach (12 oz or 350 g)
2 mandarin oranges (if not in season use canned or your favorite fruit)
1/4 cup red onion
1/4 cup crumbled feta, light
1/3 cup of your favorite dressing, fat-free
  My favorite for this salad is poppy seed.
1/4 cup cashews (optional)

<u>Serves 4-6</u>
Half the sauce will be leftover.

60 Ready, Let's Eat

Equipment List:

Large shallow oven-proof pan
Muffin tins
Cooling rack
Cutting board
Salad spinner
Colander
Large bowls
Small bowl
Fork or Electric beaters
Sharp knives
Whisk
Fork & Mixing spoons
Grater for cheese
Can opener
Measuring cups and spoons
Waxed paper

Per serving:

Calories	583
Fat	24.2 g
Protein	44.7 g
Carbohydrate	47.9 g
Fiber	4.5 g
Sodium	1110 mg

U.S. Food Exchanges:		Cdn. Food Choices:	
2 1/2	Starch	3	Carb
5	Meat-lean	4	Meat/Alt
1	Vegetable	2	Fat
1	Fat		

Assumes half the sauce is leftover.

20

WEEK 5

Prep Time

Ginger Beef with Egg Noodles and Snap Peas

Instructions:

Don't change yet! Take out equipment.

1. Heat oil in a large nonstick **fry pan** at medium heat. Finely chop garlic adding to pan as you chop. Grate ginger adding to pan as you grate. Finely chop green onions adding to pan as you cut. Saute for 2-3 minutes.

   Add beef to fry pan. Break up the beef with a spoon. Brown until no longer pink.

   Add soy sauce, vinegar, sesame oil, red pepper flakes, chili sauce and cilantro to pan once beef is cooked.

   ...meanwhile...
2. Fill a **kettle** with water and bring to a boil. Add boiling water to ginger beef fry pan then stir in **uncooked** egg noodles.
   Cover and cook over medium heat until noodles are al dente, about 7 minutes.

   ...meanwhile...
3. Slice zucchini into long wedges adding to pan as you cut. Rinse snap peas. Add to pan. Fold mixture together and heat through.

   Garnish with sliced green onion and cilantro on individual plates.

4. Serve fresh snap peas on the side.

Ingredients:

Take out ingredients.
1 tsp canola oil
6 cloves garlic
  (or 2 Tbsp fresh garlic from a jar)
1 Tbsp finely grated fresh ginger
  (or 1 Tbsp fresh ginger from a jar)
1 bunch green onions (1 cup chopped)

1 lb or 450 g extra lean ground beef
  (or use pork)

1/4 cup soy sauce, reduced-sodium
2 Tbsp rice wine vinegar
1 Tbsp sesame oil
1/2 - 1 tsp red pepper flakes
1/4 cup sweet chili sauce
2 Tbsp cilantro (optional)

3 cups boiling water

3/4 lb or 340 g broad egg noodles

1/2 of a small zucchini
1 cup snap peas

green onion (optional)
cilantro (optional)

2 cups snap peas

<u>**Serves 4-6**</u>

30 Ready, Let's Eat

Equipment List:

Large nonstick fry pan or wok
Kettle
Cutting board
Colander
Grater
Sharp veggie knife
Mixing Spoon
Measuring cups and spoons

Per serving:

Calories	396
Fat	9.4 g
Protein	25.0 g
Carbohydrate	53.5 g
Fiber	3.3 g
Sodium	531 mg

U.S. Food Exchanges:		Cdn. Food Choices:	
3	Starch	31/2	Carb
2	Meat-lean	2	Meat/Alt
1	Vegetable		
1/2	Fat		

20

WEEK 5

Prep Time

Tandoori Chicken
with Basmati Rice and Peas

Instructions:

...the night before...

Take out equipment.

1. Combine the following ingredients, in a lasagna or cake pan; mustard, ginger, cumin, coriander, turmeric, lemon juice, canola oil, chilies and yogurt. Stir until well blended.

    Make small slits with a sharp knife all over chicken pieces. Place chicken in baking pan as you slice and completely coat with sauce. Cover with plastic wrap and store in **fridge** overnight.

...when you get home...

2. Preheat **BBQ** to med (approx 350º F).
    You can do this recipe in the oven on a broiler pan as well. I often do this in the winter when I decide climbing over a snow bank to get to the BBQ just isn't worth it!

3. Place rice and water in a large microwave-safe pot with lid. **Microwave** at high for 10 minutes, then medium for 10 minutes.

...while rice is cooking...

4. Place chicken on **BBQ** grill.
    Spoon remaining sauce on chicken pieces.
    Set timer for 10 minutes. Check often.
    Flip and cook other side for the same amount of time or until inside of chicken is 180º F.

...when timer rings for rice...

5. Rinse peas in a colander.
    Place in a microwave-safe pot w/lid.
    Microwave at high for 4 minutes. Add butter if you wish.

Ingredients:

Take out ingredients.
1 1/2 tsp Dijon mustard
1 1/2 tsp fresh ginger (from a jar)
1/4 tsp cumin
1/4 tsp ground coriander
1/4 tsp turmeric
2 Tbsp lemon juice
2 Tbsp canola oil
2 Tbsp chopped green chilies
   (from a 4.5 oz or 127 mL can)
   Freeze remaining chilies for next time.
1/4 cup plain yogurt, low-fat
12-14 chicken thighs, boneless skinless
   (1 3/4 lbs or 800 g)
plastic wrap

1 1/2 cups basmati or white rice
3 cups water

prepared chicken thighs

4 cups frozen baby peas

butter (optional)

Serves 4-6

30 Ready, Let's Eat

Equipment List:

…the night before…
Large shallow baking pan
Sharp meat knife
Cutting board
Mixing spoon
Measuring cups and spoons
Plastic wrap
…when you get home…
BBQ
Large microwave-safe pot w/lid
Small microwave-safe pot w/lid
Colander
Mixing spoon
Flipper
Measuring cups

Per serving:

Calories	452
Fat	10.8 g
Protein	35.0 g
Carbohydrate	51.6 g
Fiber	4.8 g
Sodium	259 mg

U.S. Food Exchanges:		Cdn. Food Choices:	
2 1/2	Starch	3	Carb
4	Meat-lean	4	Meat/Alt
1	Vegetable		

WEEK 5

Prep Time

BBQ Salmon on a Plank, Fruit Salsa and Pita Chips

Instructions:

…the night before…
Take out equipment.
1. Soak your plank in water until you are ready to cook with it.
   …when you get home...
2. Preheat **oven** to 250º F and BBQ to 350º F.
   Spray pita pockets with cooking spray (or spritz with water).
   Sprinkle with cinnamon and sugar, then cut pitas into small triangles.
   Bake on cookie sheet. Set timer for 8 minutes.

3. Chop fruit finely adding to bowl as you cut.
   Add juice, zest, brown sugar and jelly.
   Toss to coat and let stand in **fridge**.

4. Pour apple juice into a **stove-top** pot.
   Add a squeeze of lemon juice. Bring to a full boil on high heat, then **reduce heat** to medium for a gentle boil. **Remove from heat** once reduced to about half.

   ...meanwhile...
5. Rinse the salmon thoroughly under water, then pat dry with a paper towel. On one side only, rub salmon with spices. Smear with mustard then sprinkle with brown sugar.

   Place the presoaked plank on the **BBQ** grill. Close the lid for a few minutes and keep checking until you see smoke.
   Flip the plank over and place the salmon, rub side up, on top of the charred side of plank.
   Close the lid but babysit the salmon with a squirt bottle, just in case the edges catch fire.
   Salmon is ready when it flakes off easily with a fork (approx 10-15 minutes).
   Spoon the apple juice reduction on the plates and place the cooked salmon over top.

Ingredients:

Take out ingredients.
**untreated cedar plank
  (approx 6" x 12")**

Baked Pita Chips
4-6 whole wheat pita pockets (6 1/2")
cooking spray
1/2 tsp cinnamon (for all)
1 tsp sugar (for all)

Fruit Salsa
2 Granny Smith apples
1 cup strawberries
1 kiwi fruit
juice from 1 orange
zest from 1 orange
2 Tbsp brown sugar
1 Tbsp apple or grape jelly

Apple Juice Reduction
1 cup apple juice, unsweetened
squeeze of lemon juice

2 lbs or 900 g salmon filets, boneless, skinless
paper towel
1/2 tsp coarse salt
1 tsp Mrs. Dash Original seasoning
1 tsp rosemary leaves
1/4 cup grainy Dijon mustard
2-3 Tbsp brown sugar
presoaked cedar plank

squirt bottle of water
Squirt the edges of the board if they catch fire. Lift the lid occasionally to check.

Serves 4-6

Ready, Let's Eat

98

Equipment List:

...the night before...
Cedar plank, untreated

…when you get home…
BBQ
BBQ tongs
Squirt bottle
Small stove-top pot
Cookie sheet
Cutting board
Bowl
Sharp veggie knife
Fork
2 mixing spoon
Measuring cups and spoons
Paper towel

Per serving:

Calories	407
Fat	6.5 g
Protein	34.9 g
Carbohydrate	51.8 g
Fiber	3.4 g
Sodium	644 mg

U.S. Food Exchanges:

2	Starch
4	Meat-very lean
1	Fruit
1/2	Fat

Cdn. Food Choices:

3	Carb
4	Meat/Alt

20

Prep Time

About the Recipes

Blue

This chicken is a huge hit with kids and adults. Now remember we are trying to mimic the flavor of deep fried, take-out chicken, so it's give and take for nutritional data. It may be less fat than fried chicken but it is a little higher in sodium. If you are on a sodium reduced diet omit the Italian dressing and use half the salt.

Yellow

Ron and I would go to a certain restaurant and always order this dish. I had tried to crack the recipe, but could never get it quite right. One of the moms on *Fixing Dinner* challenged me to crack it because she loved it too. I am always up for a challenge and here is the result. I was sooo excited! If you can't find sweet Indonesian soy sauce you can substitute by sweetening soy sauce with honey. Vegetarians, this is great with shrimp, and if you don't eat fish, it's also great with mixed beans and extra nuts.

Red Wings

Yum! Yum! Yum! And sooo easy!! Ron and I went out for dinner and had this amazing salmon with a citrus sauce. A few weeks later I had a really long filming weekend and when I arrived home, my beautiful husband had candles lit and this recipe in front of me with a nice glass of red. (Just one more reason to love him.)
If you are vegetarian, I sure pray you love fish!

Green

Now this is steak. The biggest mistake people make with grilling steak is that they purchase the meat way too thin. Buy a small but thick steak. This one thing can save a lot of money 'cause you have shortened the fibers of the meat both ways, so a leaner cut of meat can still be tender.
Vegetarians, I usually grill a portabella mushroom with this sauce. I stuff it with zucchini, sun dried tomatoes, Gruyere cheese and pine nuts.

Yellow Wings

This carbonara is a little different in procedure. I avoid mixing the sauce and pasta together. Our test families confirmed that it's easy to screw up a meal like this because it's one of those meals that must be served immediately. With kids that's just ridiculous. By serving the sauce over the noodles it buys you some time.
Vegetarians, use veggie bacon.

Week 6

Blue: Not Fried, Fried Chicken,
         Fresh Veggies and Dip

> Our family rating: 10
> Your family rating: _____

Yellow: Thai Chicken Noodle Salad

> Our family rating: 9
> Your family rating: _____

Red Wings: Salmon with Ron's Maple-Grapefruit Sauce,
            Mushroom Rice and Broccoli

> Our family rating: 9
> Your family rating: _____

Green: BBQ Steak with Blackberry Sauce,
         Baby Potatoes and Corn on the Cob

> Our family rating: 10
> Your family rating: _____

Yellow Wings: Fettuccini Carbonara
               with a Snap Pea Spinach Salad

> Our family rating: 8.5
> Your family rating: _____

Not Fried, Fried Chicken, Fresh Veggies and Dip

Instructions:

Take out equipment.

1. Preheat **oven** to 400° F.
    Pour the following ingredients in a medium size bowl to make a coating mix; flour, tomato cup-a-soup, dry Italian dressing mix, baking powder, paprika, salt and pepper.

    Separate egg whites from yolks and place whites in a bowl. Discard yolks.
    Roll raw drumsticks in egg white, then coating mixture.

    Spray baking pan with cooking spray.
    Place coated drumsticks on pan in lower central rack of preheated **oven**. Set timer for 50 minutes.

    …while chicken is cooking…

2. Rinse veggies you have on hand, cut and arrange on a plate.

    Serve with ranch dressing.

3. *Some people might want a starch with this. Our family likes it just this way. If you want a starch, I suggest a nice loaf of multigrain bread or bread sticks.*

Ingredients:

Take out ingredients.

Not Fried, Fried Chicken Coating
1 cup flour
1 small pouch of tomato cup-a-soup
  (3/4 oz or 21 g)
1/2 small pouch of dry Italian dressing mix
  (3/4 oz or 21 g)
1 1/2 tsp baking powder
2 tsp paprika
1 tsp salt, coarse kosher salt or sea salt
2 tsp pepper (fresh ground is best)

2 egg whites

12 chicken drumsticks
  (1 1/2 - 2 lbs or 675 - 900 g)

cooking spray I like Pam.

1 lb or 450 g celery, carrots, tomatoes, broccoli, cauliflower, cucumber, etc.
  or use precut fresh veggies, approx 4 cups
1/2 cup ranch dressing, fat-free

multigrain bread or bread sticks (optional)

Serves 4-6

60 Ready, Let's Eat

Equipment List:

Baking pan
Medium size bowl
Small bowl
Colander
Sharp veggie knife
Mixing spoon
Measuring cups and spoons

Per serving:

Calories	348
Fat	11.0 g
Protein	27.0 g
Carbohydrate	34.7 g
Fiber	2.3 g
Sodium	1123 mg

U.S. Food Exchanges:		Cdn. Food Choices:	
2	Starch	2	Carb
3	Meat-lean	3	Meat/Alt
1/2	Fat	1/2	Fat

20

Prep Time

WEEK 6

Thai Chicken Noodle Salad

Instructions:

…the night before…

Take out equipment.

1. Drizzle sesame oil into a large freezer bag. Place chicken into bag, then massage the bag so the chicken gets a thin coating of oil.

   Whisk together garlic, chili sauce, sweet soy sauce, lime juice and honey into a 2 cup measuring cup or small bowl. **Pour only 1/2 cup of the Thai dressing into the bag of chicken.** Massage the bag to coat the chicken, seal it up and lay flat in **fridge** to marinate. Store the balance of Thai dressing in **fridge** for the salad.

…when you get home...

2. Preheat **oven** or BBQ to 375° F.

3. Cook noodles according to package directions. Drain and rinse under cold water in a colander. Set aside.

   …meanwhile…

4. Spray a small cake pan with cooking spray. Discard marinade and place chicken on pan. Place in hot **oven** (or grill on the BBQ) until center of breast is 180° F (approx 10-15 minutes). Use an instant read thermometer. Slice each breast, but not all the way through, to fan over salad.

...while chicken is cooking...

5. Tear lettuce directly into salad spinner basket, rinse and spin dry.
   Sliver red onion, wash and break off cilantro leaves and smash peanuts into chunks.
   Layer each bowl or plate in this order; noodles, Romaine lettuce, red onion, mint, fanned chicken. Drizzle reserved dressing over salad then scatter crushed peanuts and fresh cilantro on top if you like. I highly recommend it!

Ingredients:

Take out ingredients.

1 tsp sesame oil
large freezer bag
4 small chicken breasts, boneless, skinless
 (1 lb or 450 g)

Thai Dressing
1 Tbsp fresh garlic (from a jar)
2 tsp or more ground fresh chili sauce
 Sambal Oelek found in Asian aisle of store.
2/3 cup sweet Indonesian soy sauce
 or mix mushroom soy sauce with honey
1/2 cup bottled lime juice
2 Tbsp honey

7 oz or 200 g steam fried egg noodles

cooking spray I like Pam.
marinated chicken

1 head Romaine lettuce
1/8 of a red onion (1/4 cup slivered for all)
1/2 cup fresh cilantro (optional)
1/4 cup salted peanuts (optional)

1 Tbsp dried mint leaves
reserved dressing

This is such a filling and delicious salad. You won't be disappointed!

<u>**Serves 4-6**</u>

Ready, Let's Eat

Equipment List:

...the night before...
Small bowl
Measuring cups and spoons
Large freezer bag

...when you get home...
Stove-top pot
Small cake pan
Cutting board
Serving plates
Salad spinner
Colander
Instant read thermometer
Sharp meat knife
Sharp veggie knife
Measuring cups and spoons

Per serving:

Calories	425
Fat	12.6 g
Protein	21.9 g
Carbohydrate	57.9 g
Fiber	3.8 g
Sodium	639 mg

U.S. Food Exchanges:		Cdn. Food Choices:	
3 1/2	Starch	3 1/2	Carb
2	Meat-lean	2	Meat/Alt
1	Fat	1	Fat
2	Fat		
	Milk		

20

Prep Time

Salmon with Ron's Maple-Grapefruit Sauce, Mushroom Rice and Broccoli

Instructions:

Don't change yet! Take out equipment.

1. Melt butter in a small, wide **stove-top** pot at med-high. Grate ginger directly into pot. Add grapefruit juice, lime juice, maple syrup and hot chili sauce. Stir and bring to a boil, then **reduce heat** to a high simmer until reduced to half. **Remove from heat.**

   …while sauce is simmering…

2. Spray a large nonstick **fry pan** with cooking spray. Wash salmon under cold water, season both sides and set aside.

3. Prepare rice according to package directions. (Cooks for approx 10 minutes.)

4. Saute salmon on one side, flip and repeat (approx 3 minutes per side). Transfer to a plate, cover tightly with foil and set aside. **Do not wash pan.**

5. Heat oil in uncleaned salmon **fry pan** at med. Wash and cut broccoli into small pieces adding to pan as you cut. Toss regularly.

   When veggies are tender but firm, reheat citrus sauce until hot.

   This dish is so amazing. The citrus sauce just keeps growing on you. Caution, you get addicted to this dish real quick!
   The broccoli ends up taking on the spices from the pan and is just delicious. We have converted more salmon haters with this dish than I can even count!

Ingredients:

Take out ingredients.

Ron's Maple-Grapefruit Sauce
1 tsp butter
1 tsp fresh ginger root
1 cup grapefruit juice, unsweetened
3 Tbsp lime juice
2 Tbsp maple syrup
1 tsp Sambal Oelek, fresh ground chili sauce (in a jar)

cooking spray I like Pam.
1 lb or 450 g salmon filets, skinless
2 tsp Mrs. Dash Original seasoning
1 tsp lemon pepper
1/2 tsp dry rosemary leaves

1 pkg mushroom rice blend, fast cooking (approx 6 oz or 165 g) or basmati rice

prepared salmon

aluminum foil

1 tsp olive oil
2-3 heads broccoli florets
  (4 cups cut and washed)

Serves 4

25 Ready, Let's Eat

Equipment List:

Large nonstick fry pan
Small, wide stove-top pot
Small stove-top pot w/lid
Cutting board
Plate
Sharp veggie knife
Grater for ginger
Mixing spoon
Measuring cups and spoons
Aluminum foil

Per serving:

Calories	348
Fat	7.3 g
Protein	29.3 g
Carbohydrate	54.6 g
Fiber	0.9 g
Sodium	120 mg

U.S. Food Exchanges:		Cdn. Food Choices:	
3	Starch	3 1/2	Carb
3	Meat-lean	3	Meat/Alt
1/2	Fruit		

15

Prep Time

W
E
E
K

6

BBQ Steak with Blackberry Sauce, Baby Potatoes and Corn on the Cob

Instructions:

Don't change yet! Take out equipment.

1. Remove steaks from fridge, sprinkle with spice on both sides and let stand at room temperature.
   I use sirloin, filet mignon, strip loin or tenderloin, depending on the occasion.
   …in the meantime…

2. Wash potatoes and place in a large **stove-top** pot of cold water. Bring to a full boil at high heat. Once boiling **reduce heat** to a low boil. Set timer for 15 minutes or until you can slide a knife into the potato easily. Drain and toss with a little butter.
   …while potatoes are cooking...

3. Add the following ingredients into a small **stove-top** pot: garlic, pepper, curry paste, red wine, jam, water and beef broth. Stir and bring to a gentle boil. Stir occasionally until reduced to half. **Remove from heat** and let stand. **Reheat just before serving.**

4. Preheat **BBQ** at med-low heat.

5. Peel back a part of the husk to ensure the corn is in good shape, then grill, husk and all, directly on **BBQ**. Turn often.
   Set timer for 8 minutes then move to upper rack or wrap in foil to keep warm.

6. **BBQ** steaks on the grill at medium-low, rotating once to create grill marks. Flip and repeat.
   Slightly under cook steaks to your preference, as they keep cooking while resting.
   Wrap in foil and let rest a few minutes.

   When ready to serve, reheat reduction then pool onto each plate. Position steak on top. Serve baby potatoes and corn on the side. I love showing the scorched husk and corn on the serving plate. I think it looks very gourmet.

Ingredients:

Take out ingredients.
3 tsp grill blend for steaks, salt free
1 tsp dried rosemary leaves
1 1/2 lbs or 675 g very thick sirloin steaks boneless, trimmed

20 baby potatoes or cut up 4 large
1 tsp butter

Blackberry Sauce
2 tsp fresh garlic (from a jar)
1 tsp fresh ground pepper
1 tsp Madras curry paste
2 Tbsp red wine
1 1/2 Tbsp blackberry jam
1/2 cup water
1 cup beef broth, reduced-sodium

4-6 corn on the cob, in husks
   You can also use corn that isn't in the husk, just wrap in foil.
aluminum foil (if no husks)
butter for corn (optional)

aluminum foil

Serves 4-6

50 Ready, Let's Eat

Equipment List:

BBQ
BBQ tongs
Large stove-top pot
Small stove-top pot
Cutting board
Sharp knife
Mixing spoon
Measuring cups and spoons
Aluminum foil

Per serving:

Calories	339
Fat	6.5 g
Protein	28.1 g
Carbohydrate	43.2 g
Fiber	5.3 g
Sodium	228 mg

U.S. Food Exchanges:	Cdn. Food Choices:
2 1/2 Starch	2 1/2 Carb
3 Meat-lean	3 Meat/Alt

15

Prep Time

WEEK 6

Fettuccini Carbonara
with a Snap Pea Spinach Salad

Instructions:

Don't change yet! Take out equipment.

1. Fill a large **stove-top** pot with water and bring to a boil for pasta.

2. Rinse spinach in basket of salad spinner and spin dry. Set aside in **fridge**.

3. Beat egg yolks lightly in a medium size bowl. Whisk in cream, milk and Parmesan cheese. Set aside.

4. Add pasta to boiling water. Drizzle olive oil into pasta water then **reduce heat** to med-high. Lift pasta to separate once it softens. Set timer according to package directions (approx 10 minutes). Drain pasta in colander and leave it there until you are ready to serve.

   ...while pasta is cooking...
   Heat olive oil in different **stove-top** pot at medium heat. Slice and crumble in bacon. Slice chives or green onion and toss into pot. Sauté slightly. **Reduce heat** to low and slowly whisk in egg mixture. Simmer, stirring occasionally.

5. Toss spinach with snap peas and any other veggies you happen to have on hand. Drizzle with your favorite salad dressing.

   When you're ready to serve dinner, rinse the noodles in very hot water, then ladle hot sauce over noodles on individual serving plates. Each person can toss their own. With kids in tow, I used to avoid making this dish the traditional way because it ended up as a goopy disaster if you didn't serve it immediately.

Ingredients:

Take out ingredients.
water

1 bag spinach (12 oz or 350 g)

3 egg yolks
1/2 cup 10% cream
1 cup 1% milk
1/2 cup Parmesan cheese, grated, light

3/4 lb or 350 g fettuccini pasta
1 tsp olive oil

1 Tbsp olive oil
8 strips fully cooked bacon
  (purchase this way)
1 Tbsp sliced fresh chives or green onion

2 cups snap peas
carrots, tomatoes, celery, etc..(optional)
1/3 cup of your favorite dressing, fat-free
I like sundried tomato dressing with this meal.

<u>Serves 4-6</u>

25 Ready, Let's Eat

Equipment List:

Large stove-top pot
Medium size stove-top pot
Mixing bowl
Colander
Cutting board
Salad spinner
Salad bowl
Sharp knife
2 large mixing spoons
Whisk or fork
Pasta fork
Measuring cups and spoons

Per serving:

Calories	438
Fat	15.6 g
Protein	20.1 g
Carbohydrate	54.4 g
Fiber	3.3 g
Sodium	614 mg

U.S. Food Exchanges:		Cdn. Food Choices:	
3	Starch	3 1/2	Carb
2	Meat-lean	2 1/2	Meat/Alt
1	Vegetable	2	Fat
2	Fat		

Prep Time

About the Recipes

Yellow

I've tried em all! I keep trying to perfect this so it's easy and healthy. As you can appreciate, with a name like butter chicken...well, that wasn't exactly easy! I loooove this recipe. It's yummy, it's quick, it's gourmet, yet down home with a twist. OK, I'll shut up now! Vegetarians, fry up some firm tofu and throw it in. It's just yum!

Red

This is a treat night meal. Some of the families found it a little spicy, while my kids are lacing it with chili flakes. So it all depends on what your family likes. If your family likes less spice cut back on the chili sauce or eliminate it altogether. Add a touch of honey if you do that. Vegetarians, purchase the veggie meatballs and do everything else the same.

Blue

This is a really great pork chop meal. I recommend purchasing an instant read thermometer for making sure the meat is a safe temp on the inside. They are inexpensive and well worth the investment! Vegetarians, try sprucing up the couscous with mixed beans, 2 Tbsp mango chutney, 2 Tbsp salsa and almonds. It's delicious and makes a great double salad meal.

Green

We did this meal on one of my shows and the kids gobbled these up! This meal is so family friendly yet attractive to serve. It's a very low calorie dinner, so don't feel bad if you feel like a little dessert later. Vegetarians, if you don't eat shrimp, try tofu and veggies.

Red

This is such a basic recipe yet so delicious. I love recipes like this. The one caution is to make sure you don't let all the broth evaporate, just most of it.
Vegetarians, saute your favorite veggies instead of the chicken, following all the same steps. When it's done top it off with a little Gruyere cheese for added protein.

Week 7

Yellow: **Butter Chicken, Basmati Rice
            and Veggie Salad**

> Our family rating: 10
> Your family rating: _____

Red: **Spicy Meatball Sandwiches with Coleslaw**

> Our family rating: 9
> Your family rating: _____

Blue: **Tomato-Cranberry Glazed Pork Chops
            with Couscous and Kinda Greek Salad**

> Our family rating: 8
> Your family rating: _____

Green: **Shrimp Brochettes in Black Bean Sauce
            with Rice and Asparagus**

> Our family rating: 9.5
> Your family rating: _____

Red: **Chicken in a Light Cream Sauce
            with Spaghetti and Broccoli**

> Our family rating: 10
> Your family rating: _____

Butter Chicken, Basmati Rice and Veggie Salad

Instructions:

Ingredients:

...the night before...

Take out equipment.

Take out ingredients.

1. Wash and chop celery, pepper and cucumber adding to a medium size bowl as you cut. Add carrots to bowl. Toss with olive oil, balsamic vinegar and spice. Cover and store in **fridge** overnight.

2 celery stalks
1 small red pepper
1/2 English cucumber
1 cup washed baby carrots
1 tsp olive oil
2 tsp balsamic vinegar
1/2 tsp Italian seasoning

...when you get home...

2. Melt butter in a large **stove-top** pot at med-high heat. Cut each breast into approx 9 chunks adding to butter as you cut. Toss until no longer pink.

1/4 cup butter

4 chicken breasts, boneless, skinless (1 1/3 lbs or 600 g) or chicken thighs which you would cut into quarters

Add garam masala, paprika, cinnamon, sugar, chili powder, Madras curry and peanut butter. Stir to coat.

1 Tbsp garam masala (spice blend) See pages 32-33 for description.
1 tsp paprika
1 tsp cinnamon
1 tsp sugar
1/2 tsp chili powder
1 Tbsp Madras curry paste
1 Tbsp peanut butter, light

Gradually stir in tomato soup, cream, milk and chicken broth. Chop cilantro and toss into pot. Stir and heat at a high simmer.

1 can tomato soup (10 oz or 284 mL)
1/2 of the soup can, filled with 10% cream
1/2 the soup can, filled with 1% milk
3/4 cup chicken broth, reduced-sodium
1/4 cup fresh cilantro

3. Combine rice and water in a large microwave-safe pot with lid. **Microwave** at high for 10 minutes, then medium for 10 minutes.

1 1/2 cups basmati rice
3 cups water
Note; a few whole cloves are a nice option to throw into the rice while it's cooking.

I suggest that you munch on the veggies while making dinner. If I am having guests over I often pick up naan bread as well. There's lots of sauce so it's great for dunking!

Serves 4-6

30 Ready, Let's Eat

Equipment List:

...the night before...
Cutting board
Salad bowl
Sharp veggie knife
Mixing spoon
Measuring spoons
...when you get home...
Large stove-top pot
Large microwave-safe pot w/lid
Cutting board
Sharp meat knife
Can opener
Mixing spoon
Measuring cups and spoons

Per serving:

Calories	500
Fat	18.9 g
Protein	27.9 g
Carbohydrate	54.9 g
Fiber	3.6 g
Sodium	586 mg

U.S. Food Exchanges:		Cdn. Food Choices:	
3	Starch	3 1/2	Carb
2 1/2	Meat-lean	2 1/2	Meat/Alt
2	Fat	2	Fat
1/2	Milk-low fat		

20

WEEK

7

Prep Time

Spicy Meatball Sandwiches with Coleslaw

Instructions:

Don't change yet! Take out equipment.

1. Combine beef, garlic, celery seed, salt and pepper together in a mixing bowl.

    Form ground beef into 1" meatballs and place in a large nonstick **fry pan** on medium heat, adding to pan as you form each meatball. *Put meatballs in the section of the pan that has the least amount of heat first!*

    In the uncleaned mixing bowl combine ketchup, chili sauce, brown sugar, Worcestershire sauce, mustard, lemon slices and water.

    Once meatballs have browned, pour sauce over top. Stir to coat. Once sauce starts to boil, **reduce heat** to a high simmer. Stir occasionally.

    …meanwhile…

2. Split rolls in half and hollow out some of the bread from both tops and bottoms, leaving edges about 1/2 inch thick.

    Slice onions (thinly) and separate into rings. Set aside.

3. Rinse coleslaw mix in colander.
    Transfer to a serving bowl.
    Toss with dressing.

    Remove lemon slices from meatball mixture before serving.
    Instant read thermometer should read 180 F.
    Serve hot meatball mixture in rolls and top with onion.

Ingredients:

Take out ingredients.

1 1/2 lbs or 675 g ground beef, extra lean
1 tsp fresh garlic (from a jar)
2 tsp celery seed
1/4 tsp ground pepper

1 cup ketchup
2/3 cup sweet chili sauce (less for less spicy
    meatball sauce)
1/4 cup brown sugar
2 Tbsp Worcestershire sauce
2 Tbsp prepared mustard
6 thin lemon slices (1/2 lemon)
1/2 cup water

6-8 small sub rolls or large hot dog buns,
    multigrain or white

1/4 red or white onion

1 lb or 450 g fresh coleslaw mix
1/2 cup coleslaw dressing, fat-free

<u>Serves 6-8</u>
(6-8 sandwiches)

30 Ready, Let's Eat

Equipment List:

Large nonstick fry pan
Small mixing bowls
Cutting board
Colander
Salad bowl
Sharp veggie knife
2 mixing spoon
Measuring cups and spoons

Per serving:

Calories	460
Fat	12.8 g
Protein	23.8 g
Carbohydrate	64.8 g
Fiber	4.2 g
Sodium	1227 mg

U.S. Food Exchanges:		Cdn. Food Choices:	
4	Starch	4	Carb
2	Meat-lean	2	Meat/Alt
1	Fat	1	Fat

WEEK 7

15

Prep Time

Tomato-Cranberry Glazed Pork Chops with Couscous and Kinda Greek Salad

Instructions:

Don't change yet! Take out equipment.

1. Preheat **oven** to 400° F.
   Combine paprika, garlic powder, thyme and pepper together in a small bowl. Sprinkle generously on both sides of chops.

   Spray a **broiler** pan with cooking spray. Place spiced chops on the broiler pan and place in hot **oven**. Set timer for 5 minutes. Flip over and cook an additional 5 minutes.

   ...while chops are cooking...

2. Combine white wine, cranberry sauce, beef broth, apple sauce, sun dried tomatoes, cranberries, vanilla and maple syrup in a small **stove-top** pot. Bring to a boil then **reduce heat** to simmer. Stir occasionally.

3. Prepare couscous in a **stove-top** pot according to package directions.

   ....meanwhile...

4. Pour olive oil, garlic, vinegar and sugar into a large salad bowl and whisk to blend.

   Cut peppers, red onion, cucumber and tomatoes, adding to salad bowl as you cut. Add feta cheese to bowl. Toss veggies until coated.

5. Remove cooked chops from broiler pan and generously brush warm glaze on both sides of the chops. Transfer chops to a serving plate and cover with aluminum foil. Inside temp should read 170° F. Let rest for 3-5 minutes before serving.

Ingredients:

Take out ingredients.

1 Tbsp paprika
1 tsp garlic powder
1/4 tsp dried thyme leaves
1/4 tsp freshly ground pepper
4-6 large thick pork chops, boneless and trimmed (1 3/4 lbs or 800 g)
   Allow more weight for bone in chops.
cooking spray I like Pam.

Tomato-Cranberry Glaze
1/4 cup white wine
1/2 cup cranberry sauce, whole berry
1 1/2 cups beef broth, reduced-sodium
2 Tbsp apple sauce, unsweetened
1 Tbsp sun dried tomatoes
1 Tbsp dried cranberries
1/2 tsp vanilla extract
1 tsp maple syrup

1 1/2 cups couscous
Optional; We like to use chicken broth for part of the liquid and right before serving we toss in chopped tomato and cilantro.

Kinda Greek Salad
2 Tbsp olive oil
1 tsp fresh garlic (from a jar)
1 Tbsp balsamic vinegar
1 tsp sugar
1/2 each of a red and green pepper
1/2 of a red onion
1/2 of an English cucumber
3 Roma tomatoes
3/4 cup light feta cheese, crumbled
1/2 cup olives (optional)

prepared glaze
aluminum foil

<u>Serves 4-6</u>

40 Ready, Let's Eat

Equipment List:

Broiler pan
2 small stove-top pots
Small mixing bowl
2 mixing spoons
Large salad bowl
Flipper
Whisk
Sharp veggie knife
Cutting board
Serving plate
Measuring cups and spoons

Per serving:

Calories	497
Fat	12.3 g
Protein	38.7 g
Carbohydrate	56.7 g
Fiber	4.9 g
Sodium	597 mg

U.S. Food Exchanges:		Cdn. Food Choices:	
3	Starch	3 1/2	Carb
4	Meat-lean	4	Meat/Alt
1	Vegetable		

WEEK 7

Prep Time

Shrimp Brochettes in Black Bean Sauce with Rice and Asparagus

Instructions:

Don't change yet! Take out equipment.

1. Preheat **oven** to 450° F.

    Lay shrimp skewers in a shallow pan.

    Pour orange juice over the skewers.
    Spread garlic sparingly over each skewer of shrimp and do the same with the ginger.
    Drizzle black bean sauce over each skewer.
    Sprinkle with brown sugar and coriander. Let stand.

2. Combine rice and water in a large microwave-safe pot or casserole dish with lid. Cover and **microwave** at high 10 minutes, then medium 10 minutes.

3. When the first 10 minute timer rings for rice, place shrimp pan in **oven** and reset timer for 10 minutes for both rice and shrimp.

    …meanwhile…

4. Wash asparagus and snap off tough end nodes. See page 34 for description.
    Place in a microwave-safe pot with lid.
    Cover and **microwave** at high for 4 minutes.
    Sprinkle with salt and butter if you must.

Ingredients:

Take out ingredients.

6-8 shrimp skewers (3/4 lb or 350 g)
You can find these in most grocery stores, but if you can't it's easy to skewer your own.
Black Bean Sauce
1 cup orange juice
1 1/2 tsp fresh garlic for all (from a jar)
1 1/2 tsp fresh ginger for all (from a jar)
1/3 cup black bean sauce
1 1/2 Tbsp brown sugar for all
2 tsp dried coriander
I prefer fresh coriander, also called cilantro, but I don't always have it on hand.

1 1/2 cups basmati or white rice
3 cups water

prepared shrimp skewers

20 asparagus spears

pinch of salt (optional)
1 tsp butter (optional)

Serves 4-6

35 Ready, Let's Eat

Equipment List:

Large microwave-safe pot w/lid
Microwave-safe pot w/lid
Shallow oven-safe pan
Colander
Measuring cups and spoons

Per serving:

Calories	286
Fat	1.4 g
Protein	17.3 g
Carbohydrate	50.2 g
Fiber	1.9 g
Sodium	697 mg

U.S. Food Exchanges:		Cdn. Food Choices:	
3	Starch	3	Carb
1 1/2	Meat-very lean	1 1/2	Meat/Alt

WEEK 7

15

Prep Time

Chicken in a Light Cream Sauce with Spaghetti and Broccoli

Instructions:

Don't change yet! Take out equipment.

1. Heat oil in a large nonstick **fry pan** at med-high. Place chicken in the pan and brown on both sides. Add garlic and chicken broth to pan. Keep simmering and flipping chicken until broth has almost evaporated.

   …while chicken is simmering…

2. Fill a large **stove-top** pot with water. Cover and bring to a boil.

3. Rinse broccoli in colander and place in a microwave-safe pot with lid. **Microwave** at high for 3 minutes. Let stand.

4. Once sauce has almost evaporated, remove chicken and set aside on a plate.
   Pour broth into the uncleaned pan and stir to deglaze (*which is a fancy way of saying getting all the brown stuff off the pan*).
   Slowly whisk in cream and sugar.
   Return chicken to pan and heat gently in the sauce.

5. Place spaghetti into boiling water and set timer according to package directions (approx 10 minutes).

   …while pasta is cooking...

6. Wash and finely chop green onion and add to chicken pan.

7. When timer rings for pasta rinse in a colander and toss with a little olive oil.
   Reheat broccoli one additional minute.

   Serve pasta, chicken and broccoli alongside each other. Pour extra cream sauce over chicken. I like hot chili flakes on mine.

Ingredients:

Take out ingredients.
1 tsp olive oil
4-6 chicken breasts, boneless, skinless (1 1/2 lbs or 675 g)
2 tsp fresh garlic (from a jar)
2 cups chicken broth, reduced-sodium

water

1 lb or 450 g broccoli florets

1/2 cup chicken broth, reduced-sodium

1 1/2 cups cream, 10%mf
1 tsp white sugar

3/4 lb or 350 g spaghetti pasta

2 green onions

1 tsp olive oil (optional)

hot chili flakes (optional)

<u>**Serves 4-6**</u>

30 Ready, Let's Eat

Equipment List:

Large nonstick fry pan
Large stove-top pot
Microwave-safe pot w/lid
Cutting board
Colander
Plate
Sharp veggie knife
Mixing spoon
Whisk
Pasta fork
Measuring cups and spoons

Per serving:

Calories	463
Fat	10.9 g
Protein	39.5 g
Carbohydrate	51.5 g
Fiber	1.6 g
Sodium	153 mg

U.S. Food Exchanges:		Cdn. Food Choices:	
3	Starch	3	Carb
4	Meat-very lean	4	Meat/Alt
1	Vegetable		
1	Fat		

15

Prep Time

About the Recipes

Red

This soup tastes like something right out of a fancy bistro. Notice that you put the cheese in the bottom of each bowl and then pour the soup on top. The cheese ends up getting stringy and it really adds to the experience! It's a vegetarian dish as long as you substitute with vegetable broth. I use reduced sodium chicken broth because vegetable broth usually has way more salt!

Green

Don't ignore this recipe if you aren't crazy about onions. The onions get super crisp so the texture is completely changed. Being that they are on the top, they are very easy to pull off as well.
Vegetarians, you are on your own tonight!

Red Wings

When the kids were little they used to think our family was weird because we would make our own pizza. They wanted to be like other families who had their pizzas delivered. Ron and I would treat the kids and ourselves (no dishes) to the boxed variety occasionally. One day when I was about to order the family pizza, as a treat, they all rebelled. They had gotten used to the ones we made at home. The teens even offered (yes, I said offered) to drive to the store and get the ingredients!

Blue

Warning, if you don't care for salmon, you may be converted after this. One of our crew members swore she would never eat salmon. After hearing us moan over countless salmon dishes, she finally took her first bite. Within weeks she proudly told me she had ordered salmon at a restaurant! Never say never!
If you are vegetarian and don't eat fish, I feel sorry for you!

Yellow

Yum! Yum! Yum! And sooo easy!! I love that you can make this in minutes! These are so delicious. If you make extra they are great to take for lunches.
Vegetarians add veggies, mixed beans, tofu or nuts to the noodles for a complete meal!

Week 8

8

Red:

Slow Cooker Southwest Soup
with Make-Your-Own Salad Wraps

Our family rating: 9.5
Your family rating: _____

Green:

Peach Glazed Chicken with Rice,
Peas and Corn

Our family rating: 9
Your family rating: _____

Red Wings:

Mediteranean Pizza with Edamame Beans

Our family rating: 10
Your family rating: _____

Blue:

Salmon with Nigerian Ground Nut Sauce,
Rice and Salad

Our family rating: 9.5
Your family rating: _____

Yellow:

Vietnamese Style Ribs
with Steam Fried Noodles and Broccoli

Our family rating: 9
Your family rating: _____

Slow Cooker Southwest Soup
with Make-Your-Own Salad Wraps

Instructions:

…the night before…

Take out equipment.

1. Heat oil in a large nonstick **fry pan** at med-high. Finely chop onion adding to pan as you cut. Cook until onion is translucent and slightly brown. Add garlic. Transfer onion and garlic to **slow cooker**.

    Drain potatoes and add to pot of slow cooker. Mash a few of the potatoes with a fork (for a natural thickener). Add chilies and salsa to pot.

    Gradually add broth.
    Add corn, tomatoes and spices. Stir until well mixed. Cover and place in **fridge**.

...in the morning...

2. Return pot with lid to slow cooker and set at **low heat**. Have a great day!

…when you get home…

3. Wash or slice any salad fixings you have on hand, and place on a serving plate.

4. Place tortillas on a serving plate and cover with plastic wrap.

5. Divide the cheese evenly among serving bowls then pour soup over cheese.

    A dollop of salsa and sour cream on top of the soup is a nice touch. Even cilantro.

    Load the tortillas with your favorite veggies and drizzle with salad dressing.

Ingredients:

Take out ingredients.
1 tsp canola oil
1 large onion
1 Tbsp fresh garlic (from a jar)

2 cans diced potatoes
  (19 oz or 540 mL each)
1 can chopped mild green chilies
  (4 1/2 oz or 125 mL)
1 cup mild, med or hot south-west salsa
  Depends on whether you like it spicy or not.

4 cups chicken broth, reduced-sodium
1 can cream corn (14 oz or 398 mL)
1 can diced tomatoes (14 oz or 398 mL)
1/2 tsp chipotle chili pepper
  (the more the spicier)
1/4 tsp curry powder

4 cups veggies: (lettuce, tomatoes, peppers, carrots, celery, snap peas etc.)

8 tortillas, 8", flour or corn
plastic wrap

1 cup sharp or old cheddar cheese, shredded, light

salsa (optional)
sour cream, fat-free (optional)
cilantro (optional)

prepared cold veggies
1/3 cup ranch dressing, fat-free
  or your favorite dressing

<u>**Serves 6-8**</u>

20 Ready, Let's Eat

Equipment List:

...the night before...
Slow cooker
Large nonstick fry pan
Cutting board
Can opener
Sharp veggie knife
Mixing spoon
Measuring cups and spoons

...when you get home...
Cutting board
Sharp veggie knife

Per serving:

Calories	368
Fat	6.3 g
Protein	14.7 g
Carbohydrate	67.2 g
Fiber	6.0 g
Sodium	1247 mg

U.S. Food Exchanges:		Cdn. Food Choices:	
3	Starch	4	Carb
1 1/2	Meat-lean	1 1/2	Meat/Alt
2	Vegetable		
1/2	Fat		

15

WEEK 8

Prep Time

Peach Glazed Chicken with Rice, Peas and Corn

Instructions:

Don't change yet! Take out equipment.

1. Preheat **oven** to 425° F.
    Spray a 9"x13" cake pan with cooking spray.
    Mix the flour and spices together in a heap on
    a piece of waxed paper.

    Cut chicken breasts into halves.
    Place chicken on the mound of spiced flour,
    lifting the sides of waxed paper to toss and
    coat. Put into sprayed pan as you coat.
    Place in hot **oven** and set timer for 10 minutes.
    When timer rings flip the chicken over and set
    timer for and additional 10 minutes.
    …while chicken is crisping…
    Thinly slice onion and set aside.

    Combine peach jam, barbecue sauce and soy
    sauce in a small bowl. Set aside.

2. Rinse peas and corn together in a colander and
    place in a small microwave-safe pot with lid.
    Microwave at high for 3 minutes. Remove
    from microwave and let stand.

3. When second timer rings for chicken, **take
    chicken out but don't turn off the oven,
    reduce heat to 350° F.**
    Scatter onion over chicken then pour sauce
    over top. Return to **oven** uncovered. Set timer
    for 30 minutes.

4. Combine rice and water in a large microwave-
    safe pot with lid. **Microwave** rice at high 10
    minutes then medium 10 minutes.

5. When ready to serve stir veggies and reheat
    for one additional minute.

Ingredients:

Take out ingredients.

cooking spray I like Pam.
1/2 cup flour
1/2 tsp pepper
1 tsp Mrs. Dash Original seasoning
waxed paper
**4 large boneless skinless chicken breasts
  (1 1/2 lb or 675 g)**

If doubling recipe, brown chicken on larger
cookie sheet and then transfer to casserole or
lasagna pan.

1 onion

3/4 cup peach jam
3/4 cup barbecue sauce
1 Tbsp soy sauce, reduced-sodium

2 cups frozen baby peas
2 cups frozen corn

1 1/2 cups basmati or white rice
3 cups water

<u>Serves 4-6</u>

60 Ready, Let's Eat

Equipment List:

9"x13" cake pan
Large microwave-safe pot w/lid
Small microwave-safe pot w/lid
Cutting board
Sharp meat knife
Sharp veggie knife
Small bowl
Measuring cups and spoons

Per serving:

Calories	525
Fat	3.0 g
Protein	35.7 g
Carbohydrate	87.7 g
Fiber	6.1 g
Sodium	395 mg

U.S. Food Exchanges:		Cdn. Food Choices:	
4	Starch	5	Carb
3	Meat-very lean	3	Meat/Alt
3	Vegetable		

15

WEEK 8

Prep Time

Mediterranean Pizza with Edamame Beans

Instructions:

Don't change yet! Take out equipment.
1. Preheat **oven** to 350° F.

2. Melt butter in a nonstick **fry pan** at med heat. Rinse edamame beans in a colander under cold water. Shake off excess water then add to pan. Sprinkle with lemon pepper and drizzle with soy sauce. Toss until skins are lightly browned and glazed. Serve in a big bowl with a side bowl for discarding shells. *If you haven't had these before you eat them like sunflower seeds.*

3. Combine olive oil, garlic and spice in a small cup.

Brush sauce evenly over pizza bases.

Layer over pizza base as you slice; zucchini, mushrooms, artichokes, sun dried tomatoes, olives, red onion, peppers, feta, mozzarella and pine nuts.

Bake in hot **oven** on separate racks on opposite sides of oven for 10 minutes.

When timer rings you may want to bubble up the cheese on **broil**.
WATCH CAREFULLY OR YOU'LL HAVE A CHARRED MESS, AND YOU'LL CRY!

You may choose to make one Mediterranean pizza and a different kind as the second pizza. Go for it. In fact it's a great way to get the family involved by having them add their own ingredients. Optional suggestions are just that, use your imagination.

Ingredients:

Take out ingredients.

Appetizer
1 tsp butter
1/2 lb or 225 g frozen edamame beans, (soybeans) in the shell
1/4 tsp lemon pepper
1 tsp soy sauce. reduced-sodium

Mediterranean Pizza Base
Sauce For 2 Pizzas
3 Tbsp olive oil
2 tsp fresh garlic (from a jar)
1/4 tsp dried basil
1/4 tsp thyme leaves
1/4 tsp rosemary
1/4 tsp oregano

2 thin crust pizza bases, 12"

Toppings For 2 Pizzas
2/3 of a small zucchini
6 mushrooms
4 artichokes hearts (from a can)
  The balance can be frozen.
10-12 sun dried tomatoes
pitted olives (optional)
1/4 red onion
1/2 red pepper
1/2 orange or yellow pepper
1/2 cup feta cheese, light
1 cup shredded mozzarella cheese, part-skim
2 Tbsp pine nuts

Regular Pizza - Optional
1/4 cup pizza sauce (jar or can)
1 tsp Italian seasoning
4-6 slices lean cooked deli ham
5 mushrooms
pineapple tidbits (from a can)

Serves 6-8

25 Ready, Let's Eat

Equipment List:

Large nonstick fry pan
Colander
Liquid measuring cup
Pastry brush
Sharp veggie knife
Cutting board
Cheese grater
Measuring cups and spoons

Per serving:

Calories	359
Fat	14.8 g
Protein	16.9 g
Carbohydrate	43.7 g
Fiber	9.4 g
Sodium	681 mg

U.S. Food Exchanges:		Cdn. Food Choices:	
1 1/2	Starch	2	Carb
2	Meat-lean	2	Meat/Alt
2	Vegetable	1 1/2	Fat
1 1/2	Fat		

15

WEEK 8

Prep Time

Salmon with Nigerian Ground Nut Sauce, Rice and Salad

Instructions:

Don't change yet! Take out equipment.

1. Combine rice and water in a large microwave-safe pot with lid. **Microwave** at high for 10 minutes, then medium 10 minutes. Let stand.

2. Heat oil in a **stove-top** pot at medium. Finely chop onion adding to pot as you cut. Sauté until translucent and just slightly brown. Add pepper, curry powder, garlic, peanut butter and broth.

   Chop tomatoes and add to pot.

   …meanwhile…

3. Spray a large nonstick **fry pan** with cooking spray and heat pan at medium high. Rinse salmon under cold water. Pat dry with paper towel and season one side. Sauté spice side down, approx 3 minutes. Season, turn and sauté other side for 3 minutes. Remove from heat, cover and let rest.

4. Sliver red pepper adding to groundnut sauce as you cut.

5. Rinse lettuce in basket of salad spinner and spin dry. Layer salad with Mandarin pieces, slivered onion and plantain chips.

   Drizzle with dressing.

   Peanuts are a great garnish.

   This meal is just amazing, quick to make and you don't need to be Nigerian to fall in love with it!

Ingredients:

Take out ingredients.
1 1/2 cups basmati rice
3 cups water

Ground Nut Sauce
1 tsp canola oil
1/2 red onion

pinch of black pepper
1/2 tsp curry powder
2 tsp fresh garlic (from a jar)
2 Tbsp peanut butter, light
1 1/2 cups vegetable broth, reduced-sodium
2 firm Roma tomatoes

cooking spray I like Pam.

4 skinless salmon filets
  (approx 1 1/2 lbs or 675 g)
paper towel
1/2 tsp garlic & herb seasoning, salt free
1/2 tsp thyme leaves

1 red pepper

1 bag cut and washed Romaine
  (12 oz or 350 g)
1 or 2 Mandarin oranges
slivered red onion (optional)
plantain chips or croutons (optional)
(plantain chips in a bag can often be found in large supermarkets)
1/3 cup of your favorite dressing, fat-free
  My favorite is poppyseed.
peanuts (optional)

Serves 4-6

40 Ready, Let's Eat

Equipment List:

Large microwave-safe pot w/lid
Large nonstick fry pan
Stove-top pot w/lid
Sharp veggie knife
Cutting board
Mixing spoon
Flipper
Salad spinner
Paper towel
Measuring cups and spoons

Per serving:

Calories	436
Fat	8.6 g
Protein	30.5 g
Carbohydrate	58.5 g
Fiber	4.5 g
Sodium	665 mg

U.S. Food Exchanges:		Cdn. Food Choices:	
3	Starch	3 1/2	Carb
3	Meat-lean	3	Meat/Alt
2	Vegetable		

20

WEEK 8

Prep Time

Vietnamese Style Ribs with Steam Fried Noodles and Broccoli

Instructions:

...the night before...
Take out equipment.
1. Place ribs in a large container with lid.

Finely chop lemon grass and transfer to a bowl. **See page 35 for chopping lemon grass.** Finely chop onion adding to bowl as you cut. Add garlic, ginger, pepper, rib sauce, water and lime juice. Whisk to combine and pour over ribs. Cover and **refrigerate**. Flip as often as you can.

...in the morning...
2. **Preheat oven to 175° F.**
Transfer ribs and marinade to an oven-proof pan. Cover with foil and cook in preheated **oven** for 8 -10 hours.
....when you get home...

3. Fill a large **stove-top** pot with water. Cover and bring to a boil at high heat. Place steam fried noodles in boiling water. Set timer for 3 minutes or follow package directions. Drain in colander and set aside.

Heat oil in the uncleaned noodle pot at med. Finely chop green onion and add to pot. Add garlic and ginger adding to pot as you cut. Add noodles to pot and toss with curry and sweet soy sauce. **Reduce heat** to low. Toss until al dente.

4. Rinse broccoli in colander. Place in microwave-safe pot or casserole with lid. **Microwave** at high for 4 minutes. Stir in spice, cover and let stand.

Serve the ribs alone or with sweet chili sauce, chopped peanuts or fresh cilantro. *You can grill the ribs on the BBQ for a few minutes to add a nice smoky flavor.*

Ingredients:

Take out ingredients.
2 1/2 lbs or 1125 g lean pork ribs, back or side
<u>**Rib Marinade and Sauce**</u>
1 stalk lemon grass
1/2 small onion
1 Tbsp fresh garlic (from a jar)
1 tsp fresh ginger (from a jar)
pinch of fresh ground pepper
1 jar strong garlic spare-rib sauce (12 oz or 341 mL) I like VH brand.
1/2 of rib sauce jar, filled with water
1 Tbsp lime juice

aluminum foil

water

1 pkg steam fried egg noodles (10 oz or 300 g)

1/2 tsp canola oil
2 green onions
1 tsp fresh garlic (from a jar)
1 tsp fresh ginger (from a jar)
drained noodles
1/4 tsp curry powder
1/4 cup Kepac Manis (sweet Indonesian soy sauce) or use mushroom soy sauce and honey

5 cups broccoli florets (1 lb or 450 g)
1 tsp mixed herb seasoning, salt free

1/4 cup sweet chili sauce (optional)
1/2 cup chopped peanuts (optional)
fresh chopped cilantro (optional)

<u>**Serves 4-6**</u>

30 Ready, Let's Eat

Equipment List:

...the night before...
Large marinade container
2 cutting boards
Mixing bowl and Whisk
Sharp veggie knife
Measuring spoons
...in the morning...
Large oven-safe pan
Aluminum foil
...when you get home...
Large stove-top pot w/lid
Large microwave-safe pot
Colander
Pasta fork and Mixing spoon
Sharp veggie knife
Measuring cups and spoons

Per serving:

Calories	622
Fat	29.7 g
Protein	31.6 g
Carbohydrate	57.0 g
Fiber	1.7 g
Sodium	513 mg

U.S. Food Exchanges:		Cdn. Food Choices:	
3 1/2	Starch	3 1/2	Carb
3	Meat-high fat	3	Meat/Alt
1	Fat	4	Fat

Assumes half of rib sauce
is discarded after cooking.

20

WEEK 8

Prep Time

About the Recipes

Red

Kids and adults will gobble this up. We use lean ground beef instead of extra lean because it's better on the BBQ. They're not as dry. Vegetarians, soak veggie grind burgers in the sauce and use a grilling tray to BBQ.

Yellow Wings

This is a really nice pasta sauce. For some reason it just looks better with bow tie pasta, not sure why, just does.
Vegetarians, this is an easy one to convert. If you eat fish, saute some salmon or white fish, then set aside. Make the sauce, place the fish pieces on the pasta and smother with sauce. If you don't eat fish, make the sauce and cover with cashews.

Green

This is one of those feel good meals that keeps growing on you.
I suggest that vegetarians roast the potatoes, slice them, then make a meal salad with nuts, beans, raisins and the roasted potatoes. Yum!!

Blue

I started using sweet potato in stew many years ago. I then tasted food from my Nigerian friends who use peanut butter in a lot of their recipes. Sometimes I use sultana raisins and sometimes I'm in the mood for dried cranberries.
Vegetarians just need to replace chicken broth with vegetable broth.

Red

When eating this brisket you will feel like you are in the south! Vegetarians, the night before, rinse then soak 1 1/4 cups dry white navy beans in 3 cups of water, in the center crock of a slow cooker. Finely chop onion and add to pot. Add 1/2 tsp each of salt, pepper, Dijon mustard and hot chilli paste. Add 1 Tbsp brown sugar, 2 tsp vinegar, 1/4 cup molasses, 1/2 cup ketchup and 2 Tbsp maple syrup. Stir and leave covered in fridge overnight. In the morning plug it in and set on low. They are perfect at 7 hours but can stay in the slow cooker a total of 9 hours if you add 1/2 cup water at the start.

Week 9

Red: BBQ Beef Satay with Steam Fried Noodles
on Mixed Greens

Our family rating: 9.5
Your family rating: _____

Yellow Wings: Orange and Mushroom Chicken
with Bow Tie Pasta and Green Beans

Our family rating: 8
Your family rating: _____

Green: Crispy Chicken
with Roasted Potatoes and Salad

Our family rating: 9
Your family rating: _____

Blue: African-Thai Stew
with Cold Veggies and Dip

Our family rating: 9.5
Your family rating: _____

Red: Southern Style BBQ Beef Brisket
with Rice and Veggies

Our family rating: 9
Your family rating: _____

BBQ Beef Satay with Steam Fried Noodles on Mixed Greens

Instructions:

...the night before...
Take out equipment.

1. Finely cut lemon grass and place in the bottom of an oven-proof rectangular casserole dish. Add peanut butter, garlic, chili sauce, ginger, honey, fish sauce and coconut milk to dish. Chop cilantro and add to dish. Whisk to combine.

   Form ground beef into 6 or 8 log shapes, approx 6 inches long and place in marinade. Turn to coat. Cover and place in **fridge**.
   ...when you get home...

2. Preheat **BBQ** to med (350° F).
   You can also bake these in the oven.
   ...meanwhile...

3. Fill a large **stove-top** pot with water, cover and bring to a boil for the noodles.

4. Place marinated beef on preheated **BBQ**. Turn occasionally to brown all sides. Inside temp should be 180° F when ready. Insert skewers when just about done.

5. Place steam fried noodles in boiling water. Set timer for 3 minutes or follow package directions. Drain in colander and set aside.

   Heat oil in a large **fry pan** at med heat. Finely chop green onion adding to pan as you chop. Add garlic and ginger and sauté slightly. Add drained noodles then toss with curry and sweet soy sauce. **Reduce heat** to low and keep tossing until heated through. Cover.

6. Rinse greens in colander and spin dry. Place greens evenly on serving plates and top with noodles. Lay beef satay over noodles.

25 Ready, Let's Eat

Ingredients:

Take out ingredients.
Marinade
1 stalk lemon grass
See page 35 for chopping lemon grass.
1/4 cup peanut butter, light
1 tsp fresh garlic (from a jar)
1 tsp Sambal Oelek (crushed chili sauce)
1/2 tsp fresh ginger (from a jar)
1 Tbsp honey
2 tsp fish sauce
1/4 cup coconut milk, light
1/4 cup cilantro

2 lbs or 900 g lean ground beef
plastic wrap or lid

water

Discard remaining marinade.

6-8 bamboo or metal skewers

12 oz or 350 g steam fried egg noodles

1 tsp canola oil
2 green onions
1 tsp fresh garlic (from a jar)
1 tsp fresh ginger (from a jar)
prepared noodles
1/4 tsp curry powder
1/4 cup sweet soy sauce (kepac manis)
  (or use mushroom soy and honey)
12 oz or 350 g prewashed mixed salad greens
peanuts and fresh cilantro
Optional toppings but they add a nice touch!

<u>**Serves 4-6**</u>

Equipment List:

...the night before...
Large shallow oven-safe pan
Cutting board
Sharp veggie knife and Whisk
Measuring cups and spoons
Plastic wrap or lid
...when you get home...
Large stove-top pot w/lid
Large nonstick fry pan w/lid
Colander
Salad spinner
BBQ tongs
Sharp veggie knife
Stirring spoon and Fork
Measuring cups and spoons
Instant read thermometer
6-8 bamboo or metal skewers

Per serving:

Calories	561
Fat	18.8 g
Protein	39.3 g
Carbohydrate	57.4 g
Fiber	2.9 g
Sodium	397 mg

U.S. Food Exchanges:		Cdn. Food Choices:	
3	Starch	3 1/2	Carb
3	Meat-lean	4	Meat/Alt
1	Vegetable	1	Fat
1	Fat		
1/2	Milk		

Assumes 1/3 of marinade discarded.

Prep Time

WEEK 9

Orange and Mushroom Chicken with Bow Tie Pasta and Green Beans

Instructions:	Ingredients:
Don't change yet! Take out equipment.	Take out ingredients.
1. Fill a large **stove-top** pot with water and bring to a boil.	**water**
2. Spray a large nonstick **fry pan** with cooking spray and heat at med-high.	**cooking spray** I like Pam.
Cut chicken into bite size pieces adding to pan as you cut. Toss until browned.	**4 chicken breasts, boneless, skinless (1 1/3 lb or 600 g)**
Reduce heat to med-low. Add oil and butter to fry pan.	**1 tsp olive oil** **1 tsp butter**
Finely chop shallot adding to pan as you cut.	**1 shallot**
Wash and slice mushrooms adding to pan as you cut. Stir and saute for 2 minutes.	**12 brown mushrooms**
Sprinkle in flour and spice. Stir.	**2 Tbsp flour** **1/2 tsp Mrs. Dash Original seasoning** **pinch of fresh pepper**
Once slightly browned add mushroom soup to pan. Fill soup can half full with chicken broth and stir in slowly until smooth.	**1 can mushroom soup (10 oz or 284 mL)** **1/2 of the soup can, filled with chicken broth, reduced-sodium (5 oz or 150 mL)**
Add orange juice, vermouth, brown sugar and baby carrots. Stir then simmer.	**1/2 cup orange juice** **1/2 cup dry vermouth** or white wine or broth **1 Tbsp brown sugar** **1 1/2 cups frozen baby carrots**
3. Place pasta in boiling water. Stir and cook following package directions (approx 10 min).	**bow tie pasta (12 oz or 350 g)**
4. Rinse beans in a colander under cold water. Place in a microwave-safe pot or casserole dish with lid. Add oyster sauce and pepper. **Microwave** at high for 4 min. Stir.	**frozen green beans (1 lb or 450 g)** **2 Tbsp oyster sauce** **black pepper to taste**
…when timer rings for pasta…	
5. Rinse the cooked pasta in colander under hot water, return to pot and toss with olive oil and basil if you wish.	**1/2 tsp olive oil** (optional) **1/2 tsp basil** (optional)
Check your sauce and make sure the carrots are tender. *Serve sauce over pasta. Parmesan is a nice touch!*	**Parmesan cheese, grated** (optional for sauce)
	<u>**Serves 4-6**</u>

25 Ready, Let's Eat

Equipment List:

Large nonstick fry-pan
Large stove-top pot w/lid
Microwave-safe pot w/lid
2 cutting boards
Colander
Sharp veggie knife
Sharp meat knife
Can opener
Mixing spoon
Measuring cups and spoons

Per serving:

Calories	505
Fat	5.4 g
Protein	36.6 g
Carbohydrate	75.2 g
Fiber	5.5 g
Sodium	484 mg

U.S. Food Exchanges:		Cdn. Food Choices:
3	Starch	4 1/2 Carb
3	Meat-very lean	3 1/2 Meat/Alt
2	Vegetable	
1	Fat	

Prep Time

Crispy Chicken
with Roasted Potatoes and Salad

Instructions:

Don't change yet! Take out equipment.

1. Preheat **oven** to 375° F.

2. Spray a large oven-safe pan with cooking spray. Unravel thighs to flatten then scrunch together to fit in pan.
Spread mayonnaise all over the tops of the chicken. Sprinkle paprika over mayonnaise. Grind fresh pepper all over.
Crush cereal in your hands and sprinkle over chicken. Place in preheated **oven**.
Set timer for 40 minutes.

3. Wash baby potatoes and place on a smaller oven-safe pan. Drizzle with olive oil and sprinkle with spice. Toss potatoes until well coated. Place in **oven** beside chicken.

4. Rinse lettuce in basket of salad spinner and spin dry.
Finely chop carrots into thin strips (julienne).

Prepare toppings and set out in small bowls.

Take out your favorite salad dressing.

Kids will love this...and you get to spend a little time with the kids, walk the dog, or whatever you wish while the oven does all the work!

Ingredients:

Take out ingredients.

cooking spray I like Pam.
10-12 chicken thighs, boneless, skinless
  (1 3/4 lbs or 800 g) or 4-6 chicken breasts
1/2 cup mayonnaise, light
1 1/2 tsp paprika
1/2 tsp fresh ground pepper
3 cups crispy rice cereal

20 baby potatoes or cut up 4 large
1 tsp olive oil
1/2 tsp garlic & herb seasoning, salt free

1 bag washed Romaine lettuce
  (12 oz or 350 g)
2 carrots

Optional Toppings
croutons, bacon bits, nuts, blueberries,
  veggies (whatever you have on hand)
1/3 cup of your favorite dressing, fat-free

Serves 4-6

50 Ready, Let's Eat

Equipment List:

Large shallow oven-safe pan
Small oven-safe pan
2 small mixing bowls
Cutting board
Salad spinner
Salad bowl
Sharp veggie knife
Spatula
Mixing spoon
Measuring cups and spoons

Per serving:

Calories	437
Fat	13.3 g
Protein	31.2 g
Carbohydrate	48.4 g
Fiber	5.6 g
Sodium	575 mg

U.S. Food Exchanges:		Cdn. Food Choices:	
3	Starch	3	Carb
3	Meat-lean	3	Meat/Alt
1	Fat	1	Fat

15

Prep Time

WEEK 9

African-Thai Stew
with Cold Veggies and Dip

Instructions:

Don't change yet! Take out equipment.
1. Heat olive oil in a large **stove-top** pot over medium heat. Finely chop onion adding to pot as you cut. Peel and cut sweet potato into cubes adding to pot as you cut.

   Dice celery and green pepper, adding to pot as you cut. *Cut and freeze the other half of pepper for next time.*
   Add garlic.
   Cook and stir for a few minutes.

   Add broth, tomatoes and drained chickpeas to pot.

   Add cumin, curry, coriander, chili, ginger, pepper and lime juice. Stir to combine and bring to a boil. **Reduce heat** to low and simmer, covered. Set timer for 25 minutes.

   When timer rings, stir in raisins and peanut butter. Simmer a few more minutes.

2. Rinse veggies and arrange on a plate.

   Rinse and chop fresh cilantro to sprinkle on top. *This is a great garnish and really kicks this dish up to the next level.*

   Leftovers freeze well if cooking for less than 6 people.

Ingredients:

Take out ingredients.
1 tsp olive oil
1 onion
1 large sweet potato (1 lb or 450 g)
 This is often mislabeled as yam.

2 stalks celery
1/2 of a small green pepper

2 tsp fresh garlic (from a jar)

3 cups chicken broth, reduced-sodium
 or use vegetable broth
1 can chunky tomatoes (19 oz or 540 mL)
 I use the spicy red pepper variety.
1 can chickpeas (19 oz or 540 mL)
1 tsp ground cumin
1 tsp curry powder
1 tsp ground coriander
1 tsp chili powder
2 tsp fresh ginger (from a jar)
1/4 tsp fresh ground pepper
1 Tbsp lime juice

1/4 cup sultana raisins (or craisons)
3 Tbsp peanut butter, light

1 lb or 450 g precut fresh veggies
1/2 cup ranch dip, fat-free (optional)

1/4 cup chopped fresh cilantro

Serves 6

35 Ready, Let's Eat

Equipment List:

Large stove-top pot
Potato peeler
Cutting board
Serving plate
Sharp veggie knife
Mixing spoon
Can opener
Measuring cups and spoons

Per serving:

Calories	366
Fat	7.3 g
Protein	16.6 g
Carbohydrate	64.2 g
Fiber	13.1 g
Sodium	623 mg

U.S. Food Exchanges:		Cdn. Food Choices:	
3	Starch	3 1/2	Carb
1	Meat-lean	1	Meat/Alt
1	Fat	1	Fat

20

Prep Time

WEEK 9

Southern Style BBQ Beef Brisket with Rice and Veggies

Instructions:

…the night before…
Take out equipment.

1. Combine Worcestershire and Liquid Smoke together in the bottom of a large cake or lasagna pan. Trim any remaining fat off brisket and discard. Place the brisket in pan and keep flipping until the brisket is saturated.

   Combine the rub ingredients in a small bowl. Sprinkle or rub spice mixture all over beef. *I use my fingers, it's just more fun.*
   Leave brisket in the pan, cover very tightly with foil and **refrigerate** overnight.

   …in the morning…
2. Preheat **oven** to 200° F.
   Transfer beef from refrigerator to oven and bake, **tightly covered**, for 8-10 hours.

   …when you get home…
3. **Reset oven** to 300° F.
   Remove beef from oven. Add BBQ sauce to drippings in pan and mix well. Slice beef thinly against the grain and return to pan as you cut. Fully coat meat with sauce. Return to **oven** until all the other components are ready to serve.

4. Place rice and water into a microwave-safe pot with lid. **Microwave** on high heat for 10 minutes, stir, and then on medium heat for 10 minutes. Let rest.

5. Rinse snap peas and carrots in a colander and place in a serving bowl.

   Brisket is a great leftover for subs!!
   If you are sending these off for lunch, wrap meat separately so the bun doesn't get soggy.

Ingredients:

Take out ingredients.
2 Tbsp Worcestershire sauce
3 Tbsp Liquid Smoke
beef brisket, trimmed (4-6 lbs or 2-3 kg)

<u>Rub Ingredients</u>
1 Tbsp dry mustard
1 Tbsp paprika
2 tsp brown sugar
1 tsp black pepper
1 tsp celery salt
1 tsp garlic powder
1 tsp onion powder
1/2 tsp cayenne pepper
aluminum foil

1/2 cup of your favorite BBQ sauce
   (a dark molasses style is best)

1 1/2 cups white rice
3 cups water

1/2 lb or 225 g snap peas
1/2 lb or 225 g baby carrots

<u>Serves 4-6</u>
Brisket makes enough for 2 meals.

30 Ready, Let's Eat

Equipment List:

...the night before....
Large cake or lasagna pan
Cutting board
Small bowl
Aluminum foil
Measuring cups and spoons
...when you get home...
Large microwave-safe pot w/lid
Serving bowl
Colander
Cutting board
Sharp meat knife
Measuring cups

Per serving:

Calories	412
Fat	9.9 g
Protein	31.5 g
Carbohydrate	47.1 g
Fiber	2.9 g
Sodium	389 mg

U.S. Food Exchanges:		Cdn. Food Choices:	
2 1/2	Starch	3	Carb
3	Meat-lean	3	Meat/Alt
1	Vegetable		

Assumes half of brisket
and sauce are leftover.

15

Prep Time

W
E
E
K

9

About the Recipes

Green

This recipe is simple yet scrumptious. It's fast and can often get kids to eat salmon, 'cause who doesn't like cheese sauce.

If you are vegetarian and don't eat fish, I suggest you slice an avocado over the hot pasta, top with cheese sauce and sprinkle with soy nuts or toasted pine nuts. I would also add some spinach to the meal for extra iron.

Red Wings

If you like butter chicken you'll love this recipe. It's not the same, but similar...and waaay easier. It's a good fake if you have no time and are craving the real thing. If you have a local store that has naan bread, it's great for dunking.

Vegetarians, either do this recipe with shrimp or seafood and if you don't eat fish, fry up some firm tofu and away you go!

Red

This is kinda traditional with an Asian twist. The sauce has a nice salty, sweet, sour and hot, but not too hot, flavor. Refrigerate left over sauce, scoop off the fat from the top once it's cold and you will really enjoy this as a bbq sauce or an add on to spruce up rice in a plain meal. The sauce can also be frozen.

Yellow Wings

Yum and Fun! These little babies are easy to make, fun to eat, deeeeeelicious and packed with nutrition...hello!

If you are vegetarian, stuff these with sauteed fish, tofu, or beans!

Blue

This meal is a really nice Chinese dinner without deep-frying.

Kids love the chicken and the adults will love the spring rolls. It's one of our fussiest dishes to make, but once you master it it's quick.

Vegetarians, skip the chicken and add tofu to the spring rolls.

Week 10

10

Green: Salmon with Cheese Sauce,
Penne Pasta and Asparagus

> Our family rating: 9.5
> Your family rating: _____

Red Wings: Madras Beef with Basmati Rice
and Broccoli

> Our family rating: 9
> Your family rating: _____

Red: Tomato-Molasses Pork Loin
with Rice and Spinach Salad

> Our family rating: 8
> Your family rating: _____

Yellow Wings: Quesadillas with Cold Veggies and Dip

> Our family rating: 9.5
> Your family rating: _____

Blue: Cheater Spring Rolls, Chicken with Cherry-
Pineapple Sauce and Stir-Fry Veggies

> Our family rating: 8.5
> Your family rating: _____

Salmon with Cheese Sauce, Penne Pasta and Asparagus

Instructions:

Don't change yet! Take out equipment.
1. Fill a large **stove-top** pot with water.
   Cover and bring to a boil.

2. Spray a nonstick **fry pan** with cooking spray.
   Wash salmon under cold water, pat dry with a
   paper towel, then season one side.

   Sauté spice side down, over med-high heat for
   approx 3 minutes.
   Season the top, turn and sauté other side of
   salmon. Cover and **remove from heat**.

   ...meanwhile...
3. Place penne pasta into boiling water and set
   timer for recommended time (approx 8 min
   or until al dente, soft on the outside and just a
   little firm on the inside).

4. Melt butter with olive oil in a small **stove-top**
   pot at medium heat.
   Add flour and whisk until smooth.
   Gradually whisk in milk and stir until sauce
   thickens slightly.
   Add cheese and cayenne. Stir. **Reduce heat to
   warm.**

5. Rinse asparagus and snap off bottom ends.
   Place asparagus and water in a microwave-
   safe pot with lid. **Microwave** at high for 5
   minutes. When timer rings toss asparagus with
   a little lemon juice and spice.

6. When pasta is ready, rinse in a colander and
   return to pot, no heat.
   Toss with a little olive oil and basil if you like.

   Drizzle cheese sauce over pasta and salmon.

Ingredients:

Take out ingredients.
water

cooking spray I like Pam.
**1 1/2 lbs or 675 g salmon filets, skinless,
   boneless** (4-6 equal pieces)
paper towel
<u>Seasoning for both sides of salmon</u>
2 tsp Mrs. Dash Original seasoning
1 tsp lemon pepper
1/2 tsp rosemary leaves

5 cups penne pasta (3/4 lb or 350 g)

<u>Cheese Sauce</u>
1 Tbsp butter
1 Tbsp olive oil
2 Tbsp flour
2 cups 1% milk

1/2 cup old cheddar cheese, light, shredded
1 Tbsp Parmesan cheese, light, grated
pinch of cayenne

20 asparagus spears
1 Tbsp water

1/2 tsp lemon juice
1/2 tsp mixed herb seasoning, salt free

1 tsp olive oil (optional)
1/2 tsp basil (optional)

<u>Serves 4-6</u>

35 Ready, Let's Eat

Equipment List:

Large stove-top pot w/lid
Small stove-top pot
Large nonstick fry pan w/lid
Microwave-safe pot w/lid
Cutting board
Colander
Sharp meat knife
Whisk
Flipper
Mixing spoon
Grater for cheese
Measuring cups and spoons
Paper towel

Per serving:

Calories	451
Fat	10.2 g
Protein	36.8 g
Carbohydrate	50.7 g
Fiber	3.3 g
Sodium	205 mg

U.S. Food Exchanges:	Cdn. Food Choices:
2 1/2 Starch	3 Carb
3 Meat-lean	3 1/2 Meat/Alt
1 Vegetable	
1/2 Milk-low fat	

WEEK 10

15

Prep Time

Madras Beef with Basmati Rice and Broccoli

Instructions:

Don't change yet! Take out equipment.

1. Combine rice and water in a large microwave-safe pot with lid.
   Cover and **microwave** at high 10 minutes, then medium 10 minutes.

2. Heat butter in a large nonstick **fry pan** or wok at med-high.
   Cut onion into slivers adding to pan as you cut. Saute until soft and slightly brown.
   Cut beef into thin short strips, against the grain, adding to pan as you cut.
   Toss occasionally until meat is no longer pink.

   Add curry paste, tomato soup and spice to pan and stir.

   Fold in yogurt.
   Stir, then **reduce heat** to a low simmer.

3. Rinse broccoli in a colander.
   Place in a microwave-safe pot or casserole with lid. Add spice and let stand.

   Remove rice from microwave to rest and pop broccoli in.

   Cover and **microwave** broccoli at high for 4 minutes, then let stand while setting the table.

   Serve beef curry beside or over rice, your choice.
   Either way, yum!!

Ingredients:

Take out ingredients.
1 1/2 cups basmati rice
3 cups water

1 tsp butter

1 onion

1 1/2 lbs or 675 g flank steak
  or lean sirloin steak

2 Tbsp Madras curry paste
1 can tomato soup (10 oz or 284 mL)
1/2 tsp garam masala (spice blend)
  See page 32-33 for spice descriptions.
1/2 tsp paprika

2 cups plain yogurt, low-fat
  can replace with sour cream

1 lb or 450 g broccoli florets
pinch of mixed herb seasoning, salt free

Serves 4-6

25 Ready, Let's Eat

Equipment List:

Large nonstick fry pan or wok
Large microwave-safe pot w/lid
Microwave-safe pot w/lid
2 cutting boards
Colander
Can opener
Sharp meat knife
Sharp veggie knife
Mixing spoon
Measuring cups and spoons

Per serving:

Calories	479
Fat	11.7 g
Protein	35.5 g
Carbohydrate	57.6 g
Fiber	2.2 g
Sodium	580 mg

U.S. Food Exchanges:		Cdn. Food Choices:	
3	Starch	4	Carb
3	Meat-lean	3	Meat/Alt
1/2	Milk-reduced fat		

WEEK 10

15

Prep Time

Tomato-Molasses Pork Loin with Rice and Spinach Salad

Instructions:

…the night before…
Take out equipment.
1. Heat oil in a large nonstick **fry pan** at medium heat. Finely chop onion adding to pan as you chop. Add garlic to pan. Saute until onions are soft and slightly brown. **Remove from heat** and set aside.

…meanwhile…
Trim off fat. Cut pork roast into 1" thick slices and place in **slow cooker.**

Pour ketchup, water, garlic powder, ground mustard, chipotle pepper, sesame oil, Worcestershire sauce and molasses over top.

Flip pork slices several times to mix and coat. Add sauteed onions and garlic to slow cooker. Cover and store center crock overnight in the **fridge**.

…in the morning…
2. Return center crock, with cover, to slow cooker and set on **low heat**.

…when you get home…
3. Combine rice and water in a microwave-safe pot or casserole. Cover and **microwave** rice at high 10 minutes, then medium 10 minutes. Let stand.

4. Rinse spinach in basket of salad spinner and spin dry.
Toss salad with your favorite salad dressing and toppings.

Note; there is lots of sauce. So save it and use it for basting chicken, fish or beef on the BBQ.

Ingredients:

Take out ingredients.
1 tsp canola oil
1 onion
2 tsp fresh garlic (from a jar)

2-3 lbs or 900-1350 g lean pork loin roast
    (or use boneless chops)

1 cup ketchup
1 1/2 cups water
1 tsp garlic powder
1 tsp ground mustard
1/4 tsp chipotle chili pepper
1 tsp sesame oil
1 Tbsp Worcestershire sauce
2 Tbsp molasses

Note
Add extra water if cooking longer than 6 hrs.
  7 hours - 1/4 cup water, 8 hours - 1/2 cup
  9 hours - 3/4 cup water, 10 hours - 1 cup

1 1/2 cups basmati rice
3 cups water

1 bag spinach (12 oz or 350 g)

1/3 cup of your favorite dressing, fat-free
Optional toppings that we looove!
  slivered red onion, crumbled feta,
  melon or mango, nuts, etc.

Serves 6.

30 Ready, Let's Eat

Equipment List:

...the night before...
Large nonstick fry pan
Slow cooker
Cutting board
Sharp veggie knife
Sharp meat knife
Large stirring spoon
Measuring cups and spoons

...when you get home...
Large microwave-safe pot
  or casserole w/lid
Salad spinner
Mixing spoons
Measuring cups

Per serving:

Calories	410
Fat	8.9 g
Protein	28.5 g
Carbohydrate	53.1 g
Fiber	2.4 g
Sodium	467 mg

U.S. Food Exchanges:		Cdn. Food Choices:	
3	Starch	3 1/2	Carb
2 1/2	Meat-lean	2 1/2	Meat/Alt
1	Vegetable	1/2	Fat
1/2	Fat		

Assumes half of sauce leftover.

WEEK 10

Prep Time

Quesadillas with Cold Veggies and Dip

Instructions:	Ingredients:
Don't change yet! Take out equipment.	Take out ingredients.

1. Preheat **oven** to 375° F.

   Heat oil in a large nonstick **fry pan** at med-low. Sliver onion adding to pan as you cut. Saute until soft and slightly brown.

   1 tsp canola oil
   1/2 onion

   Cut chicken into small bite size pieces and gradually add to pan as you cut, stirring until meat is no longer pink.

   3 chicken breasts, boneless skinless
     (1 lb or 450 g)

   Add salsa, red wine vinegar, chili powder and Worcestershire to pan and stir.

   1 cup salsa (mild, medium or hot)
   1 Tbsp red wine vinegar
   1/2 tsp chili powder
   1 tsp Worcestershire sauce

   Sliver peppers and add to pan as you cut.

   1/2 green pepper
   1/2 red pepper
   1/2 yellow pepper

2. Spray cookie sheet with cooking spray.

   cooking spray I like Pam.

   Place tortillas on a cookie sheet then bake in hot **oven** for 1 minute.

   3 soft tortillas, flour or corn, 8"

   Top each tortilla with chicken mixture, grated cheese then another tortilla.

   1 cup cheddar cheese, light, shredded
   3 more soft tortillas, 8"

   Bake in hot oven.

   Set timer for 5 minutes. *You want the top to be slightly browned and the cheese should be melted.*

   ...meanwhile...

   Chop tomatoes and slice green onions.

   3 Roma tomatoes
   3 green onions

   Slide quesadillas onto veggie board and cut into 6 pieces, like a pie.

   Serve quesadillas hot on individual plates and choose your own toppings.

   <u>Optional Toppings</u>
   salsa, sour cream, cilantro, olives, etc.

3. Serve with raw veggies and dip.

   package of cut up raw veggies, or cut your own (1 lb or 450 g)
   1/2 cup ranch dip, fat-free

   <u>**Serves 4-6**</u>

25 Ready, Let's Eat

Equipment List:

Large nonstick fry pan w/lid
Cookie sheet
2 cutting boards
Serving bowl
Sharp meat knife
Sharp veggie knife
2 mixing spoons
Measuring cups and spoons

Per serving:

Calories	362
Fat	7.0 g
Protein	30.2 g
Carbohydrate	45.8 g
Fiber	3.4 g
Sodium	944 mg

U.S. Food Exchanges:

2	Starch
3	Meat-lean
2	Vegetable

Cdn. Food Choices:

3	Carb
3	Meat/Alt

WEEK 10

Prep Time

Cheater Spring Rolls, Chicken with Cherry-Pineapple Sauce and Stir-Fry Veggies

Instructions:

...the night before...
Take out equipment.

1. Heat oil in a lge **stove-top pot or wok** at med-high. Finely chop onion adding to pan as you cut. Add ginger and garlic. Add slaw mix, soy sauce and pepper. Stir until wilted. Remove from heat, let cool, then store in **fridge**.

   ...meanwhile...

2. Cut chicken into large chunks. Toss into a freezer bag with buttermilk. Seal bag then massage to coat all pieces. Place in **fridge**.

   Combine flour, Parmesan, parsley and pepper on a large piece of wax paper. Set aside.
   ...when you get home...

3. Preheat **oven** to 375° F.
   Place oil and butter on a cookie sheet with sides. Place in oven. Once melted, remove the pan and tilt to coat entire surface.
   Remove chicken pieces from buttermilk and drop 2 or 3 at a time onto flour mixture. Pick up sides of waxed paper to coat. Place chicken onto pan then in hot oven for 30 minutes.

4. Lay 2 sheets of pastry down, long side at the bottom. Brush phyllo lightly with oil. Form a log along the bottom edge with 1/4 of the filling and begin to make a long roll folding sides in. Brush oil all over roll. Place on cookie sheet and complete 3 more rolls. Slit each roll, not cutting all the way through, to create 6 spring rolls per roll. Place on top rack of **oven** with chicken. Set timer for 20 min.

5. Spray a large nonstick **fry pan or wok** and heat at med-high. Rinse veggies in colander and add to pan.
   Add teriyaki stir fry sauce and toss until hot.

6. Combine pineapple and cherry pie filling in a microwave safe bowl. Heat sauce in **microwave** just before serving.

Ingredients:

Take out ingredients.
<u>Cheater Spring Roll Filling</u>
1 tsp canola oil
1/4 onion
1 Tbsp fresh ginger (from a jar)
2 tsp fresh garlic (from a jar)
1 lb or 450 g coleslaw mix (with carrots)
1 Tbsp soy sauce, reduced-sodium
8 twists fresh pepper
4 chicken breasts, boneless, skinless
  (1 1/3 lbs or 600 g)
1 large resealable freezer bag
1 cup buttermilk
1/3 cup flour
1/3 cup Parmesan cheese, light, grated
2 Tbsp dried parsley
8 twists fresh pepper

1 Tbsp peanut oil
1 Tbsp butter

8 sheets of phyllo pastry
2 Tbsp canola oil
prepared coleslaw filling

Optional - I love my spring rolls with
  plum sauce. I like VH brand.

cooking spray I like Pam.
5 cups frozen stir-fry veggies (1 lb or 450 g)
1/4 cup teriyaki stir-fry sauce I like VH.

1/4 cup pineapple tidbits, drained
1/2 cup light cherry pie filling
Serve cherry sauce with chicken pieces.

<u>Serves 4-6</u>

45 Ready, Let's Eat

Equipment List:

...the night before...
Large stove-top pot or wok
2 cutting boards
Sharp veggie and meat knives
Mixing spoon
Measuring cups and spoons
Freezer bag and Wax paper
...when you get home...
2 cookie sheets w/sides
Large nonstick fry pan or wok
Small microwave-safe bowl
Colander
Pastry brush and Can opener
Sharp meat knife
Mixing and stirring spoons
Measuring cups and spoons
Wax paper

Per serving:

Calories	429
Fat	14.5 g
Protein	33.5 g
Carbohydrate	42.2 g
Fiber	6.2 g
Sodium	948 mg

U.S. Food Exchanges:		Cdn. Food Choices:	
2	Starch	2 1/2	Carb
3 1/2	Meat-lean	3 1/2	Meat/Alt
1/2	Vegetable	1	Fat
1	Fat		
1/2	Fruit		

Prep Time

GROCERY LISTS

MEATS

Ground beef 90% lean (2 lbs or 900 g)
Ground beef 95% lean (1 1/2 lbs or 675 g)
4-6 chicken breasts, boneless skinless
  (1 1/2 lbs or 675 g)
Red snapper filets (1 1/2 lbs or 675 g)

DAIRY

Butter
3 eggs
Sour cream, fat-free
Milk, 1% milk fat
8 slices cheddar or Swiss cheese, light
  (optional for hamburgers)
Parmesan cheese, light, grated
Feta cheese, light
Spinach and cheese ravioli (3/4 lb or 350 g)

PRODUCE

Fresh ginger (in a jar)
Fresh garlic (in a jar) + 1 clove
Red onion (2 for 3 meals)
Onion
Green onions (1 bunch)
Tomatoes (2)
Roma tomatoes (3)
Baby carrots (1 lb or 450 g)
English cucumber (1)
Green leaf lettuce (1 head)
Red leaf lettuce (1 head)
Avocado (1 for guacamole)
Asparagus spears (32 for 2 meals)
Snow peas (10 oz or 300 g) can use frozen

DRY ESSENTIALS

Egg noodles or rice noodles (7 oz or 350 g)
White rice and wild rice blend (1 1/2 cups)
  My favorite is Canoe brand.

BAKERY

8 whole multigrain hamburger buns
8 dinner rolls (for 2 meals)

SPICES

Basil leaves
Chili powder
Cinnamon, ground
Chipotle seasoning, salt free
Cloves, ground
Cumin powder
Dry mustard
Lemon pepper
Mrs. Dash Original seasoning
Oregano leaves
Thyme leaves
Salt & Pepper

BAKING GOODS

Canola oil
Olive oil, extra-virgin
Pecans
Flour

HELPERS

Basil pesto
Maple syrup
Soy sauce, reduced-sodium
Ketchup
Mayonnaise, light
Salsa
Worcestershire sauce
Red wine vinegar
Tabasco sauce (optional for hollandaise)
Curry paste in a jar (hot)
Hot chili sauce (Sambal Oelek)
Lime juice
Lemon juice
Pineapple tidbits, unsweetened (14 oz or 398 mL)
Chicken broth, reduced-sodium (70 oz or 2.2 L)

FROZEN FOODS

Green or yellow beans (1 lb or 450 g)

OTHER

Black olives (optional for Greek salad)
Parchment paper
Toothpicks
White wine, dry (can be nonalcoholic)

Custom Grocery List

RECIPE NAME   Page

_____

_____

_____

_____

_____

MEATS

DAIRY

PRODUCE

DRY ESSENTIALS

SPICES

BAKING GOODS

HELPERS

FROZEN FOODS

BAKERY

OTHER

Grocery List Week 2

MEATS

Sirloin or prime rib roast (3 lbs or 1350 g)
Salmon filets, boneless, skinless
  (1 1/2 lbs or 675 g)
Ground beef, extra lean (1 lb or 450 g)
12-16 chicken thighs, boneless, skinless
  (1 3/4 lbs or 800 g)
Deli ham, lean, cooked (5 oz or 142 g)

DAIRY

Butter
1 egg
Milk, 1% milk fat
Cheddar cheese, light, shredded (1 cup)
Mozzarella cheese, part-skim, shredded
  (3 cups) for 2 meals
Feta cheese light, for 2 meals

PRODUCE

Red onion (1 for 3 meals)
Green leaf lettuce (1 head)
Baby spinach, 1 bag (10 oz or 283 g)
Zucchini (2 small for 2 meals)
Broccoli florets (1 lb or 450 g)
Mushrooms (15 for 2 meals)
Red pepper (1)
Orange or yellow pepper (1)
Mandarins (3)
Red grapes, seedless

DRY ESSENTIALS

Broad egg noodles (6 oz or 170 g)
Basmati rice (3 cups for 2 meals)

SPICES

Garlic & herb seasoning, salt free
Garlic powder (optional)
Italian seasoning, salt free
Mixed herb seasoning, salt free
Mrs. Dash Original seasoning
Paprika
Salt & Pepper
Seasoning salt (option for fries)

BAKING GOODS

Cooking spray, I like Pam
Olive oil, extra-virgin
Sesame oil
Powdered gravy thickener (optional for gravy)
Cashews (1/2 cup)
Pine nuts (for veggie pizza)

HELPERS

Honey
Basil pesto in a jar
Soy sauce, reduced-sodium
Pizza sauce (for ham pizza)
Cranberry juice (2 cups)
Lime juice
Pineapple tidbits, unsweetened (14 oz or 398 mL)
Cream of mushroom soup (10 oz or 284 mL)
Tomato soup (10 oz or 284 mL)
Salad dressing, fat-free, strawberry vinaigrette and
  creamy onion or your favorites

FROZEN FOODS

Baby peas (1/2 lb or 225 g)
French fries, 5 minute (1 lb or 450 g)

BAKERY

Pizza bases, thin crust (2 x 12")

OTHER

Aluminum foil

Custom Grocery List

RECIPE NAME   Page

_____

_____

_____

_____

_____

MEATS

DAIRY

PRODUCE

DRY ESSENTIALS

SPICES

BAKING GOODS

HELPERS

FROZEN FOODS

BAKERY

OTHER

RECIPE NAME

MEATS

Pork or beef ribs (2 1/2 lbs or 1125 g)
Ground beef 95% lean (1 lb or 450 g)
Chicken filets or breasts, boneless skinless
  (1 1/3 lbs or 600 g)
Sirloin steak, 2" thick (1 1/2 lbs or 675 g)

DAIRY

Butter
Sour cream, fat-free
Milk, 1% milk fat
Tex-Mex cheese, shredded (1 1/2 cups)
Cheddar cheese, light, shredded (3/4 cup)

PRODUCE

Fresh ginger (in a jar)
Fresh garlic (in a jar)
Onion (2 for 3 meals)
Red onion (1)
Baby potatoes (20 or 4 large)
Green onions (1 bunch)
Roma tomatoes (5 for 2 meals)
Cherry tomatoes (1 cup)
Celery (3 stalks for 2 meals)
Broccoli florets (1 lb or 450 g)
Red pepper (1)
Baby carrots (1/3 lbs or 150 g)
English cucumber (1)
Mushrooms (6)
Green leaf lettuce (1 head)
Spinach leaves, 1 bag (12 oz or 350 g)
Cilantro (1 1/4 cups for 3 meals)
Mandarin orange (2) optional for salad

DRY ESSENTIALS

Basmati rice (1 1/2 cups)
Couscous
Cavatappi pasta or any spiral pasta (4 cups)
Hard shell tacos (optional)

SPICES

Chili powder
Cloves
Cumin powder
Dry mustard
Garlic & herb seasoning, salt free
Italian seasoning, salt free
Chipotle seasoning, salt free
Onion flakes
Paprika
Salt & Pepper
Turmeric

BAKING GOODS

Olive oil, extra-virgin
Balsamic vinegar
Brown sugar (optional for rib rub)
Mincemeat, 1/2 cup (in a jar found with
    dessert pie fillings
Spanish peanuts (optional)
Nuts for salad (optional)

HELPERS

Maple syrup
Ketchup
Salsa, chunky
Mango chutney (option for Sweet Indian Chicken)
Curry paste in a jar (Madras)
Cream of mushroom soup (10 oz or 284 mL)
Chicken broth, reduced-sodium
  (3 cups for 2 meals)
1 can solid tuna in water (6 1/2 oz or 180 g)
Salad dressing, fat-free, poppyseed or your
  favorite

FROZEN FOODS

Baby peas (1/2 lb or 250 g)
Baby corn (1/2 lb or 250 g)

BAKERY

Tortillas, soft 10" (6 – 10)

OTHER

Aluminum foil
White wine, dry (can be nonalcoholic)

Custom Grocery List

RECIPE NAME   Page

_____

_____

_____

_____

_____

MEATS

DAIRY

PRODUCE

DRY ESSENTIALS

SPICES

BAKING GOODS

HELPERS

FROZEN FOODS

BAKERY

OTHER

RECIPE NAME	Page

MEATS

Ground beef 90% lean (2 lbs or 900 g)
Ground beef 95% lean (1 lb or 450 g)
3 chicken breasts boneless skinless (1 lb or 450 g)
1 whole roasting chicken, raw (3 lbs or 1350 g)
Scallops, fresh or frozen (5 oz or 150 g)
Shrimp, cooked, deveined (7 oz or 200 g)

DAIRY

Butter (optional)
Egg (1)
Milk, 1% milk fat
Parmesan cheese, light, grated (optional)

PRODUCE

Fresh garlic (in a jar)
Shallot (1)
Onion (2 for 2 meals)
Potatoes, baby (15–20)
Cherry tomatoes (12)
Bean sprouts (optional for wraps)
Carrots (4 large for two meals)
Celery (2 stalks)
English cucumber (1)
Red and Green pepper (1 each)
Broccoli florets (1 lb or 450 g)
Spaghetti squash (1)
Brown mushrooms (16 for 2 meals)
Green leaf lettuce (2 heads for 2 meals)
Cilantro (optional for seafood curry)

DRY ESSENTIALS

Rice stick noodles (1/4 lb or 113 g)
Penne pasta (12 oz or 350 g)

BAKERY

Foccacia bread, 1 loaf
Whole wheat tortillas 10" (6-10)
Fine bread crumbs

FROZEN FOODS

Baby peas (1 lb or 450 g)
Green beans (1 lb or 450 g)

SPICES

Cayenne (optional for Ginger Ale Chicken)
Cumin powder
Curry powder
Garam masala (if hard to find see pages 32-33)
Garlic powder
Ginger powder
Lemon pepper
Smoked paprika
Red pepper flakes (optional for pasta sauce)
Salt & Pepper
Salt, coarse

BAKING GOODS

Canola oil
Olive oil, extra-virgin
Sesame oil
Brown sugar

HELPERS

Chinese cooking wine
Balsamic vinegar (optional)
Cream of mushroom soup (10 oz or 284 mL)
Curry paste in a jar (Tandoori)
Lime juice
1 can pasta sauce (24 oz or 680 mL)
  Hunts is my favorite
1 can spicy pasta sauce (24 oz or 680 mL)
  Hunts is my favorite.
1 can diced tomatoes (14 oz or 398 mL)
1 can tomato paste (5 1/2 oz or 156 ml)
Pineapple tidbits, unsweetened (14 oz or 398 mL)
Peach jam
Peanut butter, light
Plum sauce, VH is my favorite
Salad dressing, your favorite
Salad dressing, light, Catalina
Soy sauce, reduced-sodium
Sun dried tomatoes, in oil, (in a jar)
Sweet chili sauce

OTHER

Paper towels
Aluminum foil
1 can ginger-ale (12 oz or 355 mL)

Custom Grocery List

RECIPE NAME   Page

_____

_____

_____

_____

_____

MEATS

DAIRY

PRODUCE

DRY ESSENTIALS

SPICES

BAKING GOODS

HELPERS

FROZEN FOODS

BAKERY

OTHER

RECIPE NAME	Page

MEATS

12-14 chicken thighs, boneless, skinless
 (1 3/4 lbs or 800 g)
5 chicken breasts, or thighs boneless, skinless
 (1 2/3 lb or 750 g)
Ham, ready to serve, reduced-sodium
 (3-4 lbs or 1.3-1.8 kg)
Salmon filets, boneless, skinless (2 lbs or 900 g)
Ground beef, 95 % lean (1 lb or 450 g)

DAIRY

Butter
Yogurt, light, plain (1/4 cup)
Sour cream, fat-free (3/4 cup)
Milk, 1% milk fat
Eggs (2)
Sharp or old cheddar cheese, light (3/4 cup)
Tex-Mex cheese, shredded (1 cup)
Feta cheese, light (3/4 cup)

PRODUCE

Fresh ginger (in a jar) & Fresh garlic (in a jar)
Red onion (1/4) & Green onion (1 bunch)
Red bell pepper (1)
Jalapeno pepper (1) optional for Corn Muffins
Cilantro (optional for Ginger Beef)
Potatoes, thinned skinned, (4 large)
Zucchini (1 small)
Broccoli florets (1 lb or 450 g)
Spinach, prewashed, 1 bag (12 oz or 350 g)
Snap peas (3 cups)
Apples, Granny Smith (2)
Strawberries (5)
Kiwi (1)
Orange (1) & Mandarin orange (2) or canned

DRY ESSENTIALS

Basmati rice (1 1/2 cups)
Egg noodles, broad (3/4 lb or 340 g)
Tortilla chips (optional for Tex-Mex Chicken)

BAKERY

Pita pockets, whole wheat, 6 1/2 " (4-6)

SPICES

Coarse salt & Pepper
Chipotle seasoning, salt free
Cinnamon, ground & Cloves, ground
Coriander, ground
Cumin, ground
Mrs. Dash Original seasoning
Onion flakes
Oregano leaves
Red pepper flakes
Rosemary leaves
Turmeric, ground

BAKING GOODS

Cooking spray, I like Pam
Canola oil & Sesame oil
Baking powder & Baking soda
Brown sugar & White sugar
Cornmeal
Cornstarch
Flour
Apricots, dried (1/4 cup)
Cashews (1/2 cup) optional for Salad
Rice wine vinegar

HELPERS

Dijon mustard
1 can chopped green chilies (4.5 oz or 127 mL)
1 small can creamed corn
1 can tomato sauce (14 oz or 398 mL)
 I like Hunts Italian
Apple juice (2 1/2 cups for 2 meals)
Lemon juice
Soy sauce, reduced-sodium
Sweet chili sauce
Apple or grape jelly
Salsa (you choose the heat)
Poppy seed salad dressing, light (or your favorite)

FROZEN FOODS

Baby peas (1 lb or 450 g)
Frozen corn (1/2 cup)

OTHER

Paper towel
Plastic wrap & Aluminum foil
Cedar plank, untreated (approx 6" x 12")
1 can ginger ale (12 oz or 355 mL)

Custom Grocery List

RECIPE NAME   Page

_____

_____

_____

_____

_____

MEATS

DAIRY

PRODUCE

DRY ESSENTIALS

SPICES

BAKING GOODS

HELPERS

FROZEN FOODS

BAKERY

OTHER

RECIPE NAME	Page
Not Fried, Fried Chicken, Veggies, Dip	102
Thai Chicken Noodle Salad	104
Salmon, Grapefruit Sauce, Rice, Broccoli	106
BBQ Steak, Blackberry Sauce, Potatoes, Corn	108
Fettuccini Carbonara, Snap Pea Spinach Salad	110

MEATS

4 small chicken breasts, boneless, skinless
  (1 lb or 450 g)
12 chicken drumsticks (1 1/2 lbs or 675 g)
4-6 steaks, sirloin, 2" thick or tenderloin
  (1 1/2 lbs or 675 g)
4-6 salmon filets, boneless, skinless
  (5 oz or 150 g each)
Bacon, fully cooked, 8 strips

DAIRY

Butter
Eggs (5)
Milk, 1% milk fat
Cream 10% milk fat
Parmesan, light, grated (1/2 cup)

PRODUCE

Fresh garlic (from a jar)
Fresh ginger (from a jar)
Red onion (1)
Green onion (1) or chives
Cilantro (fresh or dry)
Baby potatoes (20)
Corn on the cob (4-6) or frozen
Broccoli florets (2-3)
Romaine lettuce (1 head)
Celery, baby carrots, cauliflower, broccoli
  or packaged dipping veggies (for 2 meals)
Snap peas (2 cups)
Spinach leaves (12 oz or 350 g)

DRY ESSENTIALS

Steam fried noodles (7 oz or 200 g)
Mushroom rice blend, fast cooking, 1 pkg
  (6 oz or 165 g) or use basmati rice
Fettuccini pasta (3/4 lb or 350 g)

FROZEN FOODS

SPICES

Cilantro leaves (or fresh)
Coarse salt
Grill blend for steaks, salt free
Lemon pepper
Mint leaves (or fresh)
Mrs. Dash Original seasoning
Paprika
Pepper
Rosemary leaves

BAKING GOODS

Cooking spray, I like Pam
Olive oil, extra-virgin
Sesame oil
Flour
Baking powder
Peanuts, salted (optional for Thai Salad)

HELPERS

Lime juice
Grapefruit juice (1 cup)
Blackberry jam
Liquid honey
Maple syrup
Sambal Oelek (fresh ground chili sauce in a jar)
Kepac Manis (sweet Indonesian soy sauce)
Curry paste (Madras)
Tomato cup of soup (1 small pouch)
Dry Italian dressing mix (1 small pouch)
Ranch dip or dressing, light
Sun dried tomato dressing, light or your favorite
Beef broth, reduced-sodium (10 oz or 284 mL)

BAKERY

Multigrain bread or breadsticks
  (optional for Not Fried Chicken meal)

OTHER

Aluminum foil
Red wine (can be nonalcoholic)
Freezer bag

Custom Grocery List

RECIPE NAME   Page

_____

_____

_____

_____

_____

MEATS

DAIRY

PRODUCE

DRY ESSENTIALS

SPICES

BAKING GOODS

HELPERS

FROZEN FOODS

BAKERY

OTHER

RECIPE NAME

MEATS

Ground beef, extra lean (1 1/2 lbs or 675 g)
4-6 chicken breasts or thighs, boneless, skinless
  (1 1/2 lbs or 675 g)
8-10 chicken thighs, boneless, skinless
  (1 1/3 lbs or 600 g)
4-6 pork chops, thick (1 3/4 lbs or 800 g)

DAIRY

Butter
Cream, 10% milk fat (2 cups)
Milk, 1% milk fat
Feta cheese, light (3/4 cup)

PRODUCE

Fresh garlic (from a jar)
Fresh ginger (from a jar)
Red onion (1)
Green onion (1 bunch)
Red pepper (2)
Green pepper (1)
English cucumber (1)
Baby carrots (1 cup)
Celery (2 stalks)
Roma tomatoes (3)
Cilantro
Asparagus (20)
Broccoli florets (1 lb or 450 g)
Coleslaw mix (1 lb or 450 g)
Lemon (1)

DRY ESSENTIALS

Basmati rice (3 cups for 2 meals)
Couscous (1 1/2 cups)
Spaghetti pasta (3/4 lb or 350 g)

BAKERY

6-8 sub rolls (or hot dog buns)

FROZEN FOODS

6-8 shrimp on skewers (2 oz or 55 g each)
  or skewer your own

SPICES

Celery seed
Cinnamon
Chili powder
Coriander (cilantro) or fresh
Garam masala (spice blend see pages 32-33)
Garlic powder
Hot chili flakes (optional)
Italian seasoning, salt free
Paprika
Salt & Pepper
Thyme leaves

BAKING GOODS

Cooking spray, I like Pam
Olive oil, extra-virgin
Brown sugar
White sugar
Balsamic vinegar
Cranberries, dried
Vanilla extract

HELPERS

Chicken broth, reduced-sodium
  (3 1/2 cups for 2 meals)
Beef broth, reduced-sodium (1 1/2 cups)
Tomato soup (10 oz or 284 mL)
Apple sauce
Maple syrup
Peanut butter, light
Sun dried tomatoes (from a jar)
Ketchup
Prepared mustard
Worcestershire sauce
Sweet chili sauce
Curry paste (Madras)
Black bean sauce
Orange juice
Cranberry sauce, whole berry
Coleslaw salad dressing, light

OTHER

Olives 1/2 cup (optional for Greek salad)
White wine (1/4 cup) can be nonalcoholic
Aluminum foil

Custom Grocery List

RECIPE NAME   Page

_____

_____

_____

_____

_____

MEATS

DAIRY

PRODUCE

DRY ESSENTIALS

SPICES

BAKING GOODS

HELPERS

FROZEN FOODS

BAKERY

OTHER

RECIPE NAME	Page
Slow Cooker Southwest Soup, Salad Wraps	126
Peach Glazed Chicken, Rice, Peas, Corn	128
Mediterranean Pizza, Edamame Beans	130
Salmon, Ground Nut Sauce, Rice, Salad	132
Vietnamese Style Ribs, Noodles, Broccoli	134

MEATS

4 large boneless skinless chicken breasts
  (1 1/2 lbs or 675 g)
4 salmon filets, boneless, skinless
  (1 1/2 lbs or 675 g)
Lean pork back ribs, or side (2 1/2 lbs or 1125 g)
4-6 slices lean cooked deli ham

DAIRY

Butter
Sour cream, fat-free (optional for Wraps)
Sharp or old cheddar, light, shredded (1 cup)
Mozzarella cheese, part skim, shredded (1 cup)
Feta cheese, light (1/2 cup)

PRODUCE

Fresh garlic (from a jar)
Fresh ginger (from a jar)
Mushrooms (11)
Red onion (1) & Onion (3)
Green onions (2)
Roma tomatoes 2
Zucchini (1)
Broccoli florets (1 lb or 450 g)
Red bell pepper (2)
Yellow or orange bell pepper (1/2)
Veggies for veggie wraps (4 cups)
  (lettuce, tomatoes, peppers, etc.)
Cilantro (optional for Soup and Wraps)
Lemon grass (1 stalk)
Romaine lettuce, washed (12 oz or 350 g)
Mandarin oranges (2)

DRY ESSENTIALS

8 soft tortillas, corn or flour, 8"
Basmati rice (3 cups for 2 recipes)
Plantain chips (or croutons)
Steam fried egg noodles (10 oz or 300 g)

FROZEN FOODS

Baby peas (2 cups)
Corn (2 cups)
Edamame beans in the shell (soy beans)
  (1/2 lb or 225 g)

SPICES

Basil leaves & Oregano leaves
Chipotle chili pepper & Curry powder
Garlic and herb seasoning, salt free
Italian seasoning, salt free
Lemon pepper & Pepper
Mixed herb seasoning, salt free
Rosemary leaves & Thyme leaves

BAKING GOODS

Cooking spray, I like Pam
Canola oil & Olive oil, extra-virgin
Flour
Pine nuts & Peanuts (optional for Salmon & Ribs)

HELPERS

2 cans diced potatoes (19 oz or 540 mL each)
1 can chopped green chilies (4.5 oz or 127 mL)
1 can cream corn (14 oz or 398 mL)
1 can diced tomatoes (14 oz or 398 mL)
1 small can artichoke hearts (freeze the balance)
Sun dried tomatoes
Lime juice
Salsa (you choose the heat)
Peach jam, all fruit (3/4 cup)
Peanut butter, light
BBQ sauce (3/4 cup)
Pizza sauce (1/4 cup)
Pineapple tidbits (optional for Pizza)
Soy sauce, reduced-sodium
Sweet chili sauce
Strong garlic spare-rib sauce (12 oz or 341 mL)
  VH is my favorite
Kepac Manis (sweet Indonesian soy sauce)
Chicken broth, reduced-sodium (4 cups)
Vegetable broth, reduced-sodium (1 1/2 cups)
Ranch dressing or dip, light (1/2 cup)
Poppy seed salad dressing, light (1/3 cup)
  or your favorite

BAKERY

Pizza crusts, thin, 12" (2)

OTHER

Plastic wrap & Waxed paper
Paper towel
Pitted olives (optional for Pizza)

Custom Grocery List

RECIPE NAME   Page

_____

_____

_____

_____

_____

MEATS

DAIRY

PRODUCE

DRY ESSENTIALS

SPICES

BAKING GOODS

HELPERS

FROZEN FOODS

BAKERY

OTHER

RECIPE NAME	Page

MEATS

10-12 chicken thighs, boneless, skinless
  (1 3/4 lbs or 800 g) or 4-6 breasts
4 chicken breasts (1 1/3 lb or 600 g)
Ground beef, 90% lean (2 lbs or 900 g)
Beef brisket (4-6 lbs or 2-3 kg)
Bacon bits (optional for Salad)

DAIRY

Butter
Parmesan cheese, grated (optional for Pasta)

PRODUCE

Fresh garlic (in a jar) & Fresh ginger (in a jar)
Sweet potato (1 large) often mislabeled yam
Baby potatoes 20
Onion (1) & Shallot (1)
Green onions (2)
Green pepper (1/2)
Celery (2 stalks)
Carrots (2) & Baby carrots (1/2 lb or 225 g)
Snap peas (1/2 lb or 225 g)
Cilantro (1 bunch)
Lemon grass (1 stalk)
Mixed salad, washed (12 oz or 350 g)
Romaine lettuce, washed, 1 bag (12 oz or 350 g)
Fresh veggies, precut, (1 lb or 450 g)
Brown mushrooms (12)

DRY ESSENTIALS

Basmati or white rice (1 1/2 cups)
Bow tie pasta (12 oz or 350 g)
Steam fried noodles (12 oz or 350 g)
Crispy rice cereal (3 cups)
Croutons (optional for Salad)

OTHER

Aluminum foil
Plastic wrap
Bamboo skewers
Vermouth (1/2 cup) or white wine or broth

BAKERY

SPICES

Basil leaves (optional for Pasta)
Cayenne pepper
Celery salt
Chili powder
Cumin, ground & Coriander, ground
Curry powder
Dry mustard
Garlic and herb seasoning, salt free
Garlic powder & Onion powder
Mrs. Dash Original seasoning
Paprika
Pepper

BAKING GOODS

Cooking spray, I like Pam
Canola oil & Olive oil, extra-virgin
Flour
Brown sugar
Sultana raisins
Peanuts (optional for Satay)

HELPERS

Mushroom soup (10 oz or 284 mL)
Chicken broth, reduced-sodium (4 cups for 2 meals)
1 can chunky tomatoes (19 oz or 540 mL)
1 can chick peas (19 oz or 540 mL)
Orange juice (1/2 cup)
Lime juice
Kepac Manis (sweet soy sauce)
Fish sauce
Sambal Oelek (crushed chili sauce)
Oyster sauce
Coconut milk, light
Worcestershire sauce
Liquid Smoke
BBQ sauce, molasses style best
Peanut butter, light
Liquid honey
Ranch dip or dressing, light (option for veggie dip)
Salad dressing, fat-free, your favorite
Mayonnaise, light

FROZEN FOODS

Baby carrots (1 1/2 cups)
Green beans (1 lb or 450 g)
Wild blueberries (optional for Salad)

Custom Grocery List

RECIPE NAME   Page

_____

_____

_____

_____

_____

MEATS

DAIRY

PRODUCE

DRY ESSENTIALS

SPICES

BAKING GOODS

HELPERS

FROZEN FOODS

BAKERY

OTHER

RECIPE NAME	Page

MEATS

7 chicken breasts, boneless, skinless
  (2 1/3 lb or 1050 g) for 2 meals
Salmon filets, boneless, skinless
  (1 1/2 lbs or 675 g)
Pork loin roast, or chops (2-3 lbs or 900-1350 g)
Flank or lean sirloin steak (1 1/2 lbs or 675 g)

DAIRY

Butter
Buttermilk (1 cup)
1% milk (2 cups)
Plain yogurt (16 oz or 500 mL)
Sour cream, fat-free (optional for Quesadillas)
Feta cheese (optional for Salad)
Sharp or old cheddar cheese, light, shredded
  (1 3/4 cup for 2 meals)
Parmesan cheese, light, grated

PRODUCE

Fresh ginger (from a jar)
Fresh garlic (from a jar)
Red onion (optional for Salad)
Onions (3 for 3 meals)
Green onions (1 bunch)
Red, yellow and green bell peppers (1 of each)
Asparagus spears (20)
Broccoli florets (1 lb or 450 g)
Fresh veggies for dipping, can be cut and packaged
  (1 lb or 450 g)
Spinach leaves, 1 bag (12 oz or 350 g)
Cilantro (optional for Quesadillas)
Roma tomatoes (3)
Coleslaw mix with carrots, 1 bag (1 lb or 450 g)
Melon or mango (optional for Salad)

DRY ESSENTIALS

Penne pasta (12 oz or 350 g)
Basmati rice (3 cups for 2 meals)

BAKERY

Tortillas, 8" soft (6)

SPICES

Basil leaves (optional for Pasta)
Cayenne pepper
Chili powder
Chipotle chili pepper, ground
Garam masala (spice blend see pages 32-33)
Garlic powder
Ground mustard
Lemon pepper & Pepper
Mixed herb seasoning, salt free
Mrs. Dash Original seasoning
Paprika
Parsley leaves
Rosemary leaves

BAKING GOODS

Cooking spray, I like Pam
Canola oil & Olive oil, extra-virgin
Sesame oil & Peanut oil
Red wine vinegar
Flour
Molasses

HELPERS

Soy sauce, reduced-sodium
Ketchup (1 cup)
Worcestershire sauce
Curry paste (Madras)
Tomato soup (10 oz or 284 mL)
Salsa (you choose the heat)
Plum sauce (optional for Spring Rolls)
  VH is my favorite
Cherry pie filling, light (1/2 cup) for Cherry Sauce
Pineapple tidbits (1/4 cup) for Cherry Sauce
Teriyaki stir-fry sauce (1/4 cup) VH is my favorite
Lemon juice
Ranch dip, fat free
Salad dressing, fat free, your favorite

FROZEN FOODS

Phyllo pastry
Stir-fry veggies (1 lb or 450 g)

OTHER

Waxed paper
Paper towel
Freezer bag, large

Main Component

beef, chicken, pork, seafood, vegetarian

'cause you have an idea
of what you'd like

Prep Code

by color
for when timing is everything

Fat Content

from lowest to highest

'cause your health requires you
to watch your fat intake

Index by Main Component

Index by Main Component

Make It Vegetarian
(see About the Recipes pages for details)

Index By Prep Code

Index By Fat Content

Our Team

God - no picture on file
God has overseen our project since before we knew about it. In fact, he knew Ron and I were meant to be together and together we would help families fix dinner, one family at a time! Thank you, God, for loving me despite the fact that I can be a turkey at times. Thanks for showing us to trust in being used for your purpose, of helping the family unit reduce stress in the home and be healthy!

Photography - Lisa Fryklund
Lisa is new to this project. She is the Director of Photography for our show "Fixing Dinner" on Food Network. During principal photography of the show, she would lay down the movie camera and pick up the digital without skipping a beat, taking photos for the network. We were so impressed that we asked her to do the photography for our book. We can't believe the talent that girl has! Lisa has become a dear friend over the years as well, which tells a person a lot about her character, having to put up with me day in and day out! Lisa is an award winning cinematographer with a wide range of experience. She has travelled the world filming for Discovery, TLC, CBC, ABC, History, CMT, HGTV and National Geographic and that's just a few on a long list of projects she's undertaken.
Lisa Fryklund is the owner of her own company.
Fryklund Cinematography www.fryklund.com

Illustrations - Hermann Brandt
We were very blessed to have met Hermann a few years ago after moving to Cochrane. We weren't looking for a new illustrator, but one day, after church, we were invited to Hermann's house for lunch. Ron and I just about fell over when we saw the amazing art in his home. We then found out he was the talented artist! Hermann studied art at the Pretoria Technicon Arts School in South Africa. When you are watching *Fixing Dinner*, you will see some of his work proudly displayed in our home. Welcome aboard Hermann, we are truly blessed! Hermann is the owner of his own company.
Brandt Fine Art and Illustration www.hermannbrandt.com

Illustrations - Lorna Bennett
Lorna was the illustrator for our first three books. Many of the symbols and art you see will likely always be a part of our system. We may have moved away, Lorna, but you will always be close to our hearts. Love you, girl! Lorna is the owner of her own company.
Lorna Bennett Illustration www.lornabennett.net

Our Team

Graphic Design and Almost Everything Else
Ron Richard

Husband, friend and boss with benefits!

Ron is the man of many hats. He's the financial planner, money creator (seriously...I think he can do that sometimes), office manager, technical support provider, contract negotiator, food stylist, editor and most recently our graphic designer. Our last graphic designer made a career change. Ron had worked side by side with her overseeing all the creative design for all of our books, so he was really excited about taking on the entire job. I don't think I have enjoyed watching him tackle a job more since we started. He had a few bumps on the road, but smiled all the way through most of them! I love you honey, and you're cute!

Ron Richard is the co-owner (with me) of our own company.
Cooking for the Rushed Inc.
www.cookingfortherushed.com

Graphic Support - Kris Nielson

Kris is calm, cool and collected at all times. He was Ron's lifeline to solving graphic design problems as well as digitally processing the food images. Kris is an international award winning graphic artist as well as a published author, photographer and a certified outdoor instructor and guide.

Kris Nielson is the principal designer of his own company.
Kris Nielson Design www.krisdesign.ca

Dietitian, Diabetes Consultant - Sandra Burgess B.A.Sc.,R.D.,C.D.E.

Sandra is an enthusiastic member of our team this year! She calculated all the food exchange and food group values. Her work revolves around making diabetes something people can manage easily. She is an avid volunteer with the Canadian Diabetes Association and Inn from the Cold Society.

Sandra Burgess is a registered dietitian and a certified diabetes educator with 30 years of professional experience.

Editors at Large, Friends

What would we do without them?

A special thanks to our church family and our friends who tested recipes, gave us feedback and encouraged us.
God Bless.

Family is Everything!

A day doesn't go by without thinking about my children and how blessed I am to have them! Thanks guys for loving mom and supporting her dreams! Now that I get to see you all grown up, I also thank you for listening to at least a few things I taught you about food. All of you have taken something out of this experience.

Dougie the health nut, you still haven't figured out that artificial sweeteners and soda pop aren't good for you, but it's just a matter of time honey, it's just a matter of time! Paige, for insisting that your mom's cooking was greater than no other, and God only knows you would know, seeing I don't think I've seen you step into the kitchen more thaaaaan twice! O.K…so I'm exaggerating! Candice, for always wanting to cook with mom, your big blue eyes laughing, even when the brownies were floating in 7 cups of brown…something! Attention! Daniel is meal planning guys! Did you hear me? Daniel is meal planning! Sorry honey, I just couldn't resist. After all, weren't you the kid who swore you would eat KD and hamburgers for the rest of your life when you moved away from home! Jeffy, one of my biggest fans, which matches the guy with the biggest heart! My almost vegetarian who was always open to trying weird stuff, as long as it's not fish. Nikki, my pasta lover, homebody and organization freak! I make you pasta and you sing through dishes, what a great combo! I love how important family is to you. You make a mom proud! Courtney, the baby of the family, the child who had to stand on a chair one day at the dinner table yelling…you know…to get everyone's attention! I didn't expect you to fall in love with cooking, but it happened, you got the bug! I'm so excited!

And who could forget Aly, the most beautiful granddaughter in the world, she is like air. All she has to do is call and Ron and I turn into mush …AND GRANDMA LOVES YOU BIGGER THAN…………..

My mother in law Solange, my inspiration, my friend. Thanks for always being there for us mom. You believed when no one else did!

Mom, for having a joy in your heart when you cook!

My brothers Don and Bruce and their wives, Nik and Jane. You are my best friends. Thanks for opening your ears and always being there with lots of great advice and love! My brother Neily and my sister Janice. We don't get to see each other much, but I sure love you and I know you love me! (Janice, thanks for wearing our company apron when entertaining and not showing any signs of embarrassment, now that's true love!) …AND BY THE WAY, WISE-GUYS, COOKING TWEEZERS ARE AWESOME!!!

My best friend Glennie, and her husband Darin, what would we ever do without you? You are two of the most beautiful people I have ever known! There are very few people who know when I need a meal, a hug, a plant or good smelly soap. Only your best friends know things like this, Glennie, Jackie and Chris. Thanks for knowing (and not laughing hysterically when I tee off)!

Our extended family. Our agent Lilana Novakovich, our manager Ron Smith, our test families and Simon and Schuster for believing that we are the next best thing since sliced bread, pun intended!

A Note from Sandi

We've come a long way baby!

It's hard to imagine that it has been a little over 10 years since all of this began. The moment that Ron said, "It's just money, go for it!" There have been moments of doubt, often wondering whether we would make it financially. Wondering how we could pay for a print run and yes, at times even a mortgage payment. Ron juggled low interest rate offers back and forth, we went without, but here we are and I wouldn't change a thing!

I remember at times hearing about those overnight success stories and thinking, man we do things the long way. I remember people nay saying our ideas, publishers telling us we shouldn't print a book with color photos, and certainly not ones that hadn't been professionally food styled. (...supposedly, intelligent people want to see fake food that they will never be able to make look as good as the picture!) That we shouldn't use a left to right format, people don't like change, well welcome to the 21st century. People are sick of diets, sick of struggling through dinner and people did want change!

So here we are turning a new page in our publishing career. Simon and Schuster from New York City now publish our books. It's hard to see the page right now as my eyes just welled up (it must be my time of the month), simply thinking about all that we have been through. Although it's weird to hand over the reins, it's also exciting and refreshing knowing if we could do what we did, just Ron and I, imagine how many people we can help with a huge team behind us who also believe that people are fed up and want to learn how to manage dinner!

We hear about all the doom and gloom, how we're getting fat and how our children are getting fat. We are one of the busiest generations and work long hours between kids and work, so the last thing we need is another diet! We don't need any more doom and gloom either; there is enough of that to go around in so many other areas of life. My life's mission is to let God work through me so that maybe, just maybe, we can beat down this chore we call dinner and turn it into the most pleasurable experience of our day.

Fixing Dinner

Since the beginning of my journey, the most intriguing project has been my show *Fixing Dinner* broadcast on Food Network, American Life and Discovery Asia. The time commitment was an eye opener as I love to accomplish, then move on to the next thing. When you film a show like mine though, the procedure takes sooooo long. First you interview the family, phone them to confirm likes, dislikes and habits. I develop recipes for them, create a one month meal plan, then write the story for television, and that doesn't include filming. These families literally become a part of my life. It seemed so slow at the start because I wanted to help more people, move quicker, and get on to the next family. But in no time at all I understood the power of television. It does take a long time to help one family but the thousands of people watching who can relate to that family, on the show, are being helped through them. Now how cool is that! The blessing of our job is knowing that through meal planning a marriage may be healthier, a strained relationship may be healing, families may be spending more time together, or someone may be getting their eating act together. Wow! Meal planning is my passion, but I am such a small part of the big picture.

I want you to meet my crew, some of the most beautiful people I have come to know. We care about each other, like family and they make me look reeeeal good!
There are many people involved in the creation of the show who are not in the picture, but are just as vital to the end result. The guys at Joe Media, editors, script writer, sound technicians and the executive producers. Of course Food Network for believing this topic is truly important.

The Cooking for the Rushed series
What makes each book different?

Life's on Fire is our first week day meal planning survival guide in the Cooking for the Rushed series. It's all about moving families from take-out to eat at home easily. Our test group showed us what families want to eat in the work week and what the food needed to taste like, if a family was to stick to the plan. This book has continued to be a platform in getting people used to the idea that dinner can taste great at home and be easy! I wanted the cover to depict my life at the time; hence the name "Life's on Fire" and the cartoon cover of Paige hauling Ron away from the stove to get to a game!

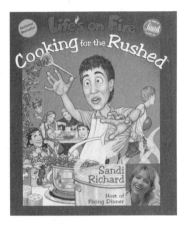

Life's on Fire is packed with delicious recipes, none exceeding a 20 minute preparation. It includes cartoons throughout the book of real life experiences with my family so you could get to know me and realize I am *Rushed*, just like you! It's packed with real photos of real food, no food styling tricks, what you see is what you eat!

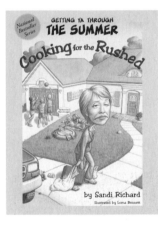

Getting Ya Through the Summer is all about how to keep the heat out of the house when the weather is hot, but it also had to be an addition to our first set of meal plans that people could use all year round. I wanted this to be our second book when I learned the following. Even though there are more fresh fruits and vegetables in the summer and the weather is perfect for outside activities, families tend to eat out more often, because it is just too hot to cook.

Getting Ya Through the Summer teaches you how to keep cooking at home, even when it's too hot! It shows you how to use the BBQ as an oven and not just a grill, how to take advantage of things like a crock pot and how to purchase healthy ingredients where someone else is doing some of the work for you. There is an additional five weeks of meal plans to add to your weekday survival guide, *Life's on Fire*.

The Healthy Family was something we felt the book trade had been missing. We are bombarded with all sorts of information about food and diets, but most of us who jump on to a diet trend, have spent less than a few hours finding out the details about it. Pairing up with two sports physicians Kelly Brett and George Lambrose (who are both passionate about their work when it comes to fitness and nutrition) was just the thing to take the medical gobbledygook (as Kelly says) and put it into lay man's terms.

The Healthy Family speaks efficiently, yet in a down home way, about all sorts of eating trends and topics so that people can spend a few minutes looking at each and understand the basics. There are an additional seven weeks of meal plans to add to your weekday survival guides, *Life's on Fire* and *Getting Ya Through the Summer*.

Let's Walk the Talk

Fundraise while encouraging families
back to the dinner table.
Let's promote great family health.

Visit
www.cookingfortherushed.com
Find out how
Cooking for the Rushed
meal planning books
can help nonprofit organizations
while bringing healthy dinners back into the home.

Online
Printable Grocery Lists
for all books

www.cookingfortherushed.com